Tales of Old Harbor

Matthew Griffin

ISBN: 978-1-7368766-0-2

Copyright © 2021 Matthew Griffin. All rights reserved.

Acknowledgements

My thanks to my father, and to my aunts and uncles for their own stories on how it was, to my cousin Steven Nickerson for access to great Aunt Eva's journal, Kat Szmit for editing, Vince Grilli for his digital prowess, and to the Burning Sky Company for Inspiration.

Table of Contents

Homeward and Mr. Kennedy 1

Bootleggers 21

6th of May 1937 37

A Day's Pay 53

The Guild Hall Supper 67

A Shanty Story 83

1st of September 1939 93

How it Was, Early 105

Emery's Tale 115

30th of October 1950 127

18th of February 1952 141

Author's Note

These are old stories, of family and of my hometown.

Griffin was historically *Gryffyng*, from Holliwell on the northeast coast of Wales. My fraternal forefathers were sea captains, as far back as the seventeenth century. My great grandfather Emery Foster Griffin left Searsport, Maine soon after the Civil War, and landed at Scatteree, Old Harbor, North Chatham, Massachusetts. He had seven children, fished, and died young; my grandfather Alexander Wayne—who was called Allie—grew up poor.

I never knew my grandfather. My one subtle memory is of him walking into the kitchen of the old house on Hitching Post Road, where I sat at the table with root beer and my grandmother's molasses cookies. He was almost ninety and tan, and he walked with a cane but still had all his teeth. The old photos of him and his fellow shoreman have a somewhat feral quality: their skin is dark from a life on the water, but their eyes and teeth are very white and overexposed. Their faces look amused and half-mad, as if the land, air, and water have permanently skewed the pH balance of their expression with all that sun and salt.

Allie served in the Navy during the Great War, married Elizabeth Blankenship from Spruce Street in Brockton, and raised a family through the Great Depression. He played the trombone and made a decent way on the piano, so he founded the Chatham Band with George Goodspeed. They performed at the dedication of the Sagamore Bridge. He saw two of his sons off to World War II and was a past commander of American Legion Post 253.

A stranger at a taphouse in town told my brother and I, once we were introduced, and he recognized our family name:

Your grandfather was the only man I've ever met that could drink, dance, play piano, sing and smoke a cigarette all at the same time.

My grandfather was a fisherman, but his true talent was storytelling. I have drank, danced, and smoked with merit in my day, but I can neither sing nor play piano. I've heard a lifetime of his stories from my parents, aunts, uncles, cousins, strangers, and friends of old. Stories of the neighborhood—of Old Harbor—and the characters who lived there, who were his contemporaries, family, and friends. I sit at the end of the farthest limb of my generational branch of the family tree. I have a heritage to upkeep, a provincial duty to my own contemporaries, and to all who enjoy a good story. They are the most powerful form of entertainment, no matter what form they take. But I don't fancy myself much of a story*teller*, so here are a few written words. A family pastoral now three generations in its telling.

Homeward and Mr. Kennedy

He moved fast for a small man, and he left footprints in the grass all the way to the southern bound of the Great Hill estate, which was closest to the sea and unkept and descended in an impassable slope to the shore. The grass was still very green despite the season and the low light. It was a dark afternoon, and made darker by the rainclouds overhead. The small man stood and watched the promontory shoreline of heavy black rocks, and the moving sea that broke against it. The southwest wind gusted with a tenor note into his ear. There was a low drum of thunder to the east.

He wanted to see the shore and the sea before his drive to the city, and the long ride home with Mr. Joseph Kennedy.

He turned up the collar of his British khaki driving coat and walked downhill as the first evening raindrops tapped his shoulders. He put his hands in the front pockets of the coat which was new and heavy, and his pockets fell halfway up his forearms. With his gloves, and the cap on his head, he'd stay dry the entire drive home.

Detached to the southwest from the grand hall of the estate were the servants' quarters, and under the porchlight were the two old Negro gardeners in from the city. They shook the raindrops off their suits in an amusing shuffle--both being old. One hurried inside, likely in dire need of the lavatory. The other stood on the small porch and ran a finger around the tip of his cap and flicked away the moisture.

The old boys came to the estate on weekends. The small man saw them on occasion, once a month at least for a year and more, and they always spoke: about the weather, or music, rum, and baseball. One of them was Anson and the other Montgomery, but the small man could never keep straight which name belonged with whom, because they were always together, and never called each other by name. Always two of them, and they worked in one of the greenhouses throughout the premises of Great Hill, which had palm trees and fruit trees, and rose and rhododendron gardens. The small man knew that both of them worked one garden exclusively because they were the very best at what they did.

The estate wasn't segregated, which was a fine thing.

The small man took his duffel bag from where he left it under the porchlight. The old boy held the door half open. The one who was Anson or Montgomery was tall and his hair and his beard were grey and smartly barbered. He looked down at the small man; the whites of his eyes were bronze.

That's some jacket.

The small man stretched his arms out in front of him and smiled wide.

Homeward and Mr. Kennedy

Wouldn't ye say? Almost as good as oilskins in this weather.

Best keep it out the rain, now. The damp'll stay with ye all night.

Yeah. Right. I'll try.

Watcha drivin' tonight?

Pierce-Arrow. The '20, I think.

Mmm. That's some automobile.

Yeah. Yeah, she's a little hard to navigate but she's good in a straight line.

Got the night shift?

Yeah, in a way.

The Pierce-Arrow was a Model 32, modified with finery to the seats and doors, and custom upholstery and specifically optioned frosted glass on the rear window. She was absolute luxury: heavy, and a handsome grey and polished nickel, and she set just inside the second double doors of the car port.

The small man pressurized the fuel system, set the rich/lean mixture on the main jet of the carburetor, primed the intake, advanced the spark of the ignition and stepped on the starter button. She came to life quickly, and the small man smiled again. She had close to forty horsepower in her, and the lights of the Model 32 were high up and set close together. He'd see well, and she had four-wheel mechanical brakes and rear leaf springs, so she'd stop under throttle when she had to.

If the rain subsided, and he kept the tires clean, the ride across all the low country to home might not be so long.

The driveway was an uncrowded cul-de-sac and he set the brake perpendicular to the front walkway that led to the great door of the hall. The small man moved outside and around the bonnet to the passenger door. He lit a cigarette. The rain was light and fell straight downwards. He kept his hands in his jacket pockets and his head down. His driving cap kept the rain off his face. The cigarette burned slow between his lips and it was a fine smoke standing there in the rain.

With the world as dim as it was, with the estate, and the stone baronial hall and the weather and the shore, it was all familiar and he was well-outfitted, as if he were still enlisted, and still in England.

He smiled and blew smoke into the rain.

Hurry up and wait...

He didn't wait long.

Galen Luther Stone walked out from behind the great door of his Tudor hall, and under the gaslights he was shadowed with an umbrella and a proper black bowler atop his head. An attaché case was under one arm. He approached the coach and closed the umbrella and nodded quick at the small man who held open the door of the Pierce-Arrow. Stone's eyes were bright and sad-looking. The white symmetry of his moustache was unrivaled.

Homeward and Mr. Kennedy

How are we this afternoon, Allie?

Fine fine, Mr. Stone. Bit damp wouldn't ye say?

Where is your umbrella, my boy?

Allie didn't answer. He didn't know where his umbrella was.

This hat and jacket do me fine, Mr. Stone.

Allie's older brother Arthur had gotten him the job at the Great Hill estate when the war let out, when there was no money to home on the water. Allie learned early that Mr. Stone was a capable man, who knew best how to prosper in the time he was given. His boats and his gardens won trophies. He put a large number of folk to work with good jobs, and he paid fair wages. (There were twenty other men in the quarters where Allie lived: groundskeepers, masons, messengers and random tradesmen. The staff who ran the interior of the hall might have been double their lot.) Allie rarely spent time inside the hall, but when he was called upon it was always to the library, which was comfortable and not like other parts of the hall which made you feel the need to whisper and keep your hands off of every stationary object on the tables and walls. The dark-wooded bookshelves of the library went nearly floor to ceiling; there was heraldry on the walls and most endtables had ashtrays and fine ceramic bottles upon them. The fireplace was black marble and seemed lit the year entire. It smelled heavy and sweet in the library, a mix of firesmoke and fresh unlit tobacco.

Allie drove out through the north iron gate. Once underway he opened her up and the Model 32 rode smooth on the well-graded state road towards the city.

Stone didn't speak up much at all on the ride to Brookline. He sat with his legs crossed and a ledger before him. He had a pen in his hand but he didn't write. He was of the world of ledgers and ink, but the light was too dim to read, and the road was hell on penmanship. When Allie slid the car along the curved driveway towards his towering Colonial, Galen Stone exited the car on his own accord.

I have the door, Allie. Thank you.

It was nighttime in Boston, and the clouds and the drizzle darkened all of it. Allie waited at the given address nearest a streetlamp, and smoked to keep away the stale redolence of the city, which was there before you drove in and there on your clothes when you left it. The city was sodden, earth and air.

Mr. Kennedy walked down the slick brick steps with a blonde girl on his left arm, and a darker stranger on his right; all were clad in the highest of fashion. The pretty girls smiled, and their lips and cheeks and noses were flush from either or both the damp and the drink. Kennedy parted their company, and the girls took the arm of the other and raced across the quiet city street. As Allie closed the door to the Pierce-Arrow he heard the click of their heels on the pavement and their laughter.

He drove out of the city, as quickly as the roads allowed.

Homeward and Mr. Kennedy

Kennedy removed his hat but kept his fur coat about his shoulders. The fresh carnation on the lapel was very white. He removed his glasses and polished them with a handkerchief. For a time he just polished in the dark, and squinted with his glasses off. He wore a half-smile and his teeth were white and Allie thought he had a face very much like an Irishman should. He kept quiet, the way Stone had. Allie figured that's how men act when their lives are spent being driven anonymously towards and away from a great many places. Kennedy didn't speak until the canal, where the bridge was up; there was time to see through the rain the two passing cabin lamps of a tugboat heading west, and bound southward.

There were gaps in the bridge and Allie drove slow and thought himself lucky not to lose a tire. The suspension of the Pierce-Arrow wasn't engineered for drawbridges and more than once both men came off their seat. Once across, the Old King's Highway was soggy and pitted and the ride was made slower.

What's your name fella?

Alexander, Mr. Kennedy, but ye best call me Allie if ye want a response.

Well, it seems your doin' me a bit of a favor.

Nah, just work Mr. Kennedy. I was headin' Capeward anyway, just not in so fancy a car.

How long ye been workin' for Stone?

A bit over a year. Older brother got me the job. Mostly I run n' maintain his boats. Seems he thinks I do just as well on land.

Treats ye well, does he?

Yessir. Mr. Stone's a helluva nice man. I tell folks t' home that I got a fresh uniform for every day o' the week and a grey suit if there's work on Sunday, and they take me for half-foolish. Hell, these shoes are only the second new pair I've ever owned.

Kennedy smiled.

Your second?

Yessir. First was issued to me by the US Navy.

You're a Navy boy?

Yessir.

See time did ye?

Yessir. USS North Dakota.

Hm. Where?

The lamps of the Model 32 fought the rain as it caught the breeze from the east, but they were high-mounted so Allie saw the road well and could speak easy enough while he drove.

Chesapeake Bay, mostly, at the end. Guarding sea lanes. Guantanamo Bay, Panama, Mexico. Most o' the Gulf ports. Supplied service detachments, we did.

Ye ever cross?

Homeward and Mr. Kennedy

Yessir, on the Henderson. A dozen times or so, I'd say. Then I got the Spanish flu and that knocked me out fer a few months. S'pose I'm lucky, though. Lost my younger brother to it last winter. Almost a year ago.

Kennedy braced himself far back in the seat.

So ya sail, do ya?

Hell Mr. Kennedy I grew up on sails. That's all there was growin' up, and that wasn't that long ago. I remember the first motored vessel I ever saw. What a cussed racket she made.

Kennedy laughed.

You from the Cape?

Yessir. North Chatham.

Allie turned his head slightly from the road.

Ye know Mr. Kennedy, this ain't the first time we've met.

Is that right?

Yessir. This past summer, at the races.

Wait now—

Kennedy leaned forward.

Weekend before the Fourth?

Yessir.

I'll be damned. Was it—

The races.

Hm. You ran Stone's—

Yessir. Twenty-one foot class.

Kennedy laughed.

Did we speak?

Not what I'd call a conflab Mr. Kennedy. Just a handshake, really.

Well, ya beat some good boats. And good captains.

If ye say so.

Ya get a bit o' the purse?

Oh, yessir. Mr. Stone's as generous as they come.

Kennedy leaned back again.

That's very true. There's nothin' about his philanthropy that's false.

I'd work for 'em 'til my dyin' day but I got a boat t' home comin' my way. I'd like to be home. On the water.

I'll have a house out here some day, soon.

Not seen a lot o' the Cape up this way t'be honest. It's pretty, the trees and marshes and all.

I'll have something right on the water.

Homeward and Mr. Kennedy

Out my way there's some trees, but nothin' like this. Ye can see how much nothin' there is when ye look at it from the water. Not much of nothin' from Stage Harbor t' Stellwagen.

Ye married?

Nossir.

Siblings?

Yessir. Five countin' m' dead brother.

No children?

Allie stifled laughter.

Nossir.

I have three, now. Some day I'll give 'em all a million dollars. They can succeed on their own or make an ass outta themselves.

Allie thought a million dollars was a lot of money for one person.

That'd be a nice thing to do.

My oldest is real smart. He's still young, but he's smart. He's gonna be president one day.

Wouldn't that be somethin'.

Ye a Democrat?

Doesn't much matter t' me either way.

Kennedy nodded.

It's not much further, now.

The Pierce-Arrow breached the drive through a square set of iron-wrought gates and a lamp from the long front porch windows shone down into the damp of the driveway. There was something of an echo from inside the house. Music and laughter.

Kennedy put his case in his lap and set his hat upon his head. His hand went deep into an inside pocket.

Allie held the door and when Kennedy stepped out they shook hands in the rain, and something passed from one to the other.

Best o' luck to ya then, Allie.

Yessir, Mr. Kennedy. Ye do the same. You n' yers. And good luck with the whole presidency bit.

The terrain along the Old King's Highway was blurred by the rain on the windscreen and Allie was lucky the windows stayed down to keep the fog and condensation off the inside glass. It was tiresome, the ride, alone, and in the quiet. When he crossed into town he had passed only a single car.

Home was the northeast corner of town, Old Harbor: shire-like, with fields extending in their entirety to the water, where Minister's Point divided the surrounding coves to the west and the east.

Allie's father Emery Foster G_____ was a sea-captain out of Searsport, Maine and legendary spar-maker. He sailed

Homeward and Mr. Kennedy

alone from the old homestead in Stockton Springs, his vessel laden with every household good he owned, and the cat. His wife Saluda Burgess, their son Arthur and three daughters Lulu May, Eva, and Ida arrived in Old Harbor by steamboat. Three years later Allie was the first child born to them in the house on Old Wharf Road. Another sister Marion and brother Emery followed. The Captain died when Allie was seven, and Saluda married the Captain's first cousin—Allie's great uncle's grandson Frank Benjamin, the postmaster—who Allie never took well to: with his dark Welsh features and sharp moustache, his low countenance and the odd pale stare of his glass eye.

Thayer's Hill was rutted with mud, and the lamps of the Pierce-Arrow faced downward. Every white house looked spectral in the periphery of their light, as if they floated off their foundations among the fields and the dark and the rain. Allie parked off the road. His home looked dark when he took his duffel bag and shut the door, but then there was yellow light from the kitchen, and the shadow of his mother in the open door of the back entryway.

It was late in the night and his mother didn't want to shout. She hissed and hurried her words.

Get in here, get in here!

Allie strode past her and through the door. Then the hissing again.

Take… take that coat off before ye go any further.

Allie doffed his cap. Saluda took hold of his jacket and she sagged a bit by its weight. She turned her back and walked into the kitchen.

Them shoes, too.

Allie crouched and untied his shoes, dulled by the rain. It was late. He felt a relief after the long ride. It was late and he was unsure if he was tired.

Ye got any tea, Ma?

I can't have tea this late!

He stood with his shoes in his hand. Both knees popped loudly and that was his only response.

Saluda shook the coat and hung it up on a high peg in the entryway and turned out the pockets to let the warm air dry them.

But I can make some… if ye like.

Thanks.

I'm puttin' yer cigarettes and matches on the table… or you'll ruin 'em, leaving 'em in these pockets. Everything else I'll—

Allie heard the contents of his pockets drop onto the table.

The kitchen was dim with the entryway lamp. Allie knew how time away from home affected the way he thought of it. He perceived the differences first, and it took time to get

Homeward and Mr. Kennedy

comfortable. There was a smell of damp wood from the rain, and the creak of the chair was especially loud so late at night.

You... You staying all weekend?

No, Ma. I gotta be back early mornin' Sunday.

Saluda busied herself with the tea.

That's an awful long drive, just for a day.

It's not that long.

Well, ye should get out an' see yer sisters. Yer sisters would like to see you.

Allie looked down at his crumpled packet of Chesterfields and the fold of bills on top of it. It was a sturdy fold, no matter the denomination.

That yer car? That looks like a... fancy car.

No, Ma! Hell I betcha that's ten year's salary.

Saluda placed a cup and saucer on the table.

I hear from Arthur. He says yer all busy, yer all workin' hard. I hear from Arthur more often than not.

The water steamed in the kettle.

Ye could write yerself ye know?

Allie stared at the folded money and tapped his forefinger on top of it.

It's hard puttin' words together in my head. Had trouble enough fillin' them tiny postcards to ya when I was overseas.

Well, ye talk well enough, don't ye? Can't see why ye can't write once in a while. Arthur's written. Arthur's always written.

I ain't in the Navy anymore, Ma. It's not like I'm that far--

Yer sisters ask for ye all the time.

Lulu May lived in Marion, not far from where Allie lived on the Great Hill estate. She married William Tucker, and had a son William Wentworth who was in school. Eva lived across the street from Saluda, in a big white house on Old Harbor Road, unmarried. Ida married Joseph Atkins Nickerson and lived near where Old Harbor met the Stony Hill Road. Marion was the youngest of them, and lived in California, where she said it never rained.

I'll hop across the street and see 'em in the morning.

Both Allie and Arthur lived off-Cape in Marion. Emery had died in the V.A. hospital in Brooklyn. Now Saluda's boys were all away.

They miss you, yer sisters.

Allie felt a cramp in his backbone and was tired suddenly. He didn't want the tea, but he stretched and sat, lit a cigarette, and took his billfold from the table to the bottom of his trouser pocket.

He would have a vessel of his own very soon.

Homeward and Mr. Kennedy

It's all well an' good for a time Ma. Nothin' enough to keep me away for long.

From the journal of Eva Parks (Griffin) Watts

Sun Jan 21 1934

Cloudy with a little snow, temp 30, clearing later in the day. Wrote to Ida Breen and Lee Rich. Home all day. Allie in for a while. Ma broke false teeth.

Mon Jan 22 1934

A nice day--SE wind and temp around 30. Washed and dried clothes. Took Ma's teeth to be fixed by Dr. Fuller. Went to bring Willie home from work tonight and we got out of gas by Orleans Road. Norman Eldredge brought some up for us after I phoned for some from Joe Kelley.

Sun Jan 28 1934

A raw south wind with temp 40 and cloudy turning to rain in PM. Capt. John Wescott of Old Harbor C.G. came over and had a chicken dinner with us which he enjoyed. We had a nice visit with him, and he went back to station at 4 p.m. We took him to East Orleans and C.G. car met him there.

Mon Jan 29 1934

Some change in weather today. It cleared in night and temp dropped just to 10 above this A.M. at 4:30 with a NW gale. Still dropping and now (10:30) down to 6 above. Went down to zero at 9 P.M. and stayed there till morning and Wayne and Bob came up here and slept, as it was so cold upstairs in their home. Allie in for by-d-by at supper time.

Tues Jan 30 1934

Wind still blowing from NW and zero this morning. Went to 20 and now (4:30 pm) down to 10 above. Clear, and still the wind NW. Pres. Roosevelt's birthday, and he 52 years old. Ida in a while this P.M. Letter from Gracie telling about her coming trip to Florida. Temp dropped to 8 above at bed time. Wayne and Bob slept here again.

Wed Jan 31 1934

Temp. 2 below at 7 AM 12 above at 9 AM. Clear, and a very light wind. Harbor frozen way across, and no water to be seen at 7 AM. Never saw it that way before.

Bootleggers

The house was empty, and all there was to do that day was wait for nightfall. The exchange always happened after nightfall, by the shore, where the men of the neighborhood of Old Harbor met with the Bostoners in darkness. It's how it was, for years.

Allie began that morning with his pipe and tea made too strong; the open pages of the *Standard Times* began to quiver by the end of his second cup. Allie considered his hands as Joe Nickerson came through the kitchen door with his pipe and a mug and his own paper under one arm. He paused at the threshold.

You heard?

Allie stood, crossed his arms, stilled his hands, and nodded.

Yuh, this mornin'.

They the same fellas? Them that's comin'?

Mmhmm.

That him ye talked to?

No. Gunny called early.

Hmm. Gunny, he--

Yuh. Ye know how it is with him, Joe. Ye know... all that money. Been some time since the repeal o' that Volstead Act and all, so...

What's the name o' the fella that does all the talkin'?

Uhh, Cruck... Cruickshank.

Boy... that's a name.

I'd say.

When?

Like always. After sundown.

Joe set his newspaper down next to Allie's, curled his jacket around the back of the chair nearest to the window, and set himself up at the table.

Well...

He chose a copy from the two in front of him.

...Ida's gone up with th' boys to Marion, so...

Allie paced the floor that morning back and forth, the same five steps between the table and his front door; his brother-in-law sat with the *Standard Times* laid open in front of him. They stood and sat and didn't speak. Allie glanced downward over Joe's shoulder, to the small picture on the facing page of some parade of tawny uniformed men with rifles, led by those who rode horses in armor. The horsemen held banners and flags that rippled overhead from halberd poles. Every horse and rider and those who marched looked made and ready for war.

I talked to Eddie Clayton, Joe. Did I tell ya?

Joe's eyes never moved from the picture.

Hmm. I guess not.

Eddie went to Boston to see Charles Lindbergh speak, ye know.

Yeah. Heard he was all over Europe. Some sort o' dip-lo-matic bit I guess.

Allie resumed his five-step back and forth.

Said Lindbergh met up with that Goering character.

Hmm.

Said that Chancellor's gettin' the whole country to work.

Joe turned the page.

I hear they's in as bad a depression as we are. Worse even.

Eddie says Lindbergh saw all sort o' things. Seems they're bent on remakin' a military.

Hmm. Ye wouldn't figure they'd want to go through all that again.

All this fightin'. Christ, Joe, why's everyone gotta be fightin' all the time?

They waited alone together, morning through afternoon, until there was no false light inside the kitchen, only late, broken Spring motes darkened by a moving shadow of oak tree branches in the wind. Allie considered the dark and made for the lamp, when there were three quick knocks on the door. The low sun was at the back of the figure there, but Allie knew it was Bert Baker because of the shadow-shape of the hat on his head.

Come ahead, Bert! Bring yer dory!

Bert stood in the entryway with a cigarette and his tin cup. He heard an absent racket of young boys, no music from the radio, nor the gentle notes of Eliz at the piano. He took a tentative step forward, as if not to disturb the quiet of the house.

Family up the church, Allie?

Nah. Lizzie's taken t' Brockton. I guess Eva got a' hold of a Buick somewhere so they headed off with m' youngest.

Joe?

Ida's up t' Marion. Boys are out t' the North Beach camp.

To Bert's left was the pantry door. He looked to Allie and tilted his head twice in its direction.

Well, then. I'd say it'd be a good a' time as any to check on the progress of the stirrings. Wouldn't ye say, Allie?

Allie rubbed his hands together and looked from Bert to Joe and back again.

Speakin' o' which, she went off just this mornin'.

Allie kept a five-gallon still kettle underneath the bottom shelf in the rear corner of the pantry, three-quarters filled with alcohol and a mash of apple cores, cranberries, corn, and when Eliz made potatoes, Allie took the peelings.

Dicky was small and dallied quietly about the kitchen that morning with his father, when a disturbance came from inside the pantry: a sound from the corner like the unclogging of some occluded hatchway.

G-G-GAruuuuuung.

Dicky turned his head towards the pantry, paused, then spun around to face his father. His small face wrinkled into a smile. He began to bounce at the knees, and he laughed and pointed at the kettle. When wee Arlen toddled into the kitchen, he scooted over to his older laughing brother so they could laugh and point together in the way small children do at the sound of anything remotely flatulent. Allie smiled, amused by his boys, both bath-scrubbed, their hair fine and damp and parted, dressed in their Sunday best on a Friday morning.

Eliz. walked into the kitchen and the laughter, smartly dressed for Brockton. The dark coat and red scarf she wore complimented her pale skin and her black hair. She took Arlen by one hand. Dicky wagged her other, and pointed again towards the pantry.

Momma, what's in Daddy's bucket?

Allie held his smile and kept his eyes downward. He needn't look to his wife to perceive the expression she wore.

Eliz. turned her eyes sideways towards her husband, before she led her sons out the door.

Just you never mind.

Allie mulled over Bert's question, then opened the pantry door.

Try a bit o' the old nervene?

Bert smoked his cigarette.

A touch o' the O Be Joyful?

Joe stood up from the table.

A little Bye-D-Bye?

Bert and Allie got down on their knees and pulled the full kettle from underneath the bottom shelf in the rear corner of the kitchen pantry. Allie removed the ceramic top and Bert procured the ladle, scraped back the scum congealed on the brim, dipped deeply into the brew beneath and drank.

Bert exhaled. His eyes watered and went red.

Ahhh. Vittles n' drink!

They ladle went around to all of them once, and over their breathing there was tapping and voice at the door. Old

Hezekiah Doane was on the front stair, crouched as low as he could get without being prone to the ground. He held the door open just enough for Allie to see his face. Hezzie's eyes were far apart and his mouth and mustache were in a half-formed O because Hezzie was old. Allie shook his head. It was very much like Hezzie to over embellish.

Chrissakes Hezzie get up off the floor.

Hezzie stood up and wiped his hands on his dungarees and fit his floppy flat cap back atop his pointed head. He spoke in a loud whisper, as if he were anxious, hesitant, half in his cups, or a merger of all three.

Allie! I hear there's alcohol on the north shore!

Allie held open the door with a stiff arm, and the old man walked under it.

I know ALL ABOUT IT.

Hezzie met with the others as Bert slid the kettle back to its corner. Bert felt fresh and flushed and warm, and wiped a hand down a white chin beard tinged ocher with tobacco stain. Allie put on a light jacket and was the last of them out of the house. It was late in March and nighttime, and the moon rose. Outside they could see their breath. There was no wind. The reedy wail of the tiny frogs in the grasses by the salt pond surrounded them. Their sound was cathartic, and the men didn't speak. Four of them walked to Scatteree, where Bill Speight stood alone in the dark. Bill lived atop Cotchpinicut Road, and the shanties were closer than Allie's house. In his right hand was a spade half-planted in the soft soil. He spun around it like a dance partner when the men approached. Bill was a bundle of nerves, but he collected himself and presented the spade handle forward in acknowledgement.

I ain't got a gun.

Allie shook his head again and looked to Joe.

Ain't we an awkward squad.

They heard the city men before they saw them. Whatever it was they drove idled high as it rolled down Stony Hill Road in low gear and came to a halt after the turn at the salt pond. The new green blades of beachgrass overhanging the way to the shore caught the lights of the truck, and the men lost their night vision. The truck set there unmoving for a long moment, then it bucked forward, as if the driver was unsure and misshifted. It moved slow and hesitant along the grass and the dark towards them.

Joe was the largest man among them, and the other four shoremen stood at each other's shoulders behind him. Bill chopped his spade into the sand over and over again in the same spot: *Clumpclumpclumpclumpclump.*

Christ that looks like Arthur Gould's truck, don't it?

It was a Ford model with a covered bed, and very much like the truck in which Arthur Gould hauled rubbish. It was unassuming, a worktruck, and could have belonged to any of them.

Allie knew who it belonged to.

Bill, I can promise ye that ain't Arthur.

The sky was clear and dark enough for stars. The driver cut the lights of the truck and came to a halt a few yards from the half-circle of men. The driver never left his seat, nor his hands the steering wheel. An enormous well-dressed passenger exited from the right side. One hand held open the door of the truck, the other held a Thompson M1921 with a finger off the trigger.

Cruickshank slid out from between the others. He was properly dressed: a white collared shirt and brimmed hat. He smoked packet cigarettes and wore a polished watch on his left wrist. He was courteous and direct, both traits Allie found atypical of a city man.

The two men tread carefully, as if mistrustful of the beachsand.

Those of Old Harbor were indifferent to it all. They looked like poor men, with their ill-fitted jackets and heavy trousers with many folds tucked into their boots. All wearing a different shaped cap of a unique faded color. Their faces darkened by a life on the shore.

Allie moved first and offered his hand.

Mr. Cruickshank.

Evenin' gentlemen. What's yer name, fella?

Allie.

The two shook hands.

Allie.

Cruickshank took the cigarettes from his waist coat and with a hospitable flick of his wrist proffered a Pall Mall to the small man in front of him.

So... where is it?

Allie took the cigarette, packed it three times on the knuckle of his thumb, and pointed crossways over his shoulder to the east.

It's right out there. I'll take ye to it.

Allie was a small man, but Cruickshank looked smaller. The edge of his voice dulled, and he wore an ill-favored look.

Really? Why... Why ain't it on shore?

Allie beckoned with a short motion and strode towards the skiff set near the waterline of the harbor.

I'll take ye to it.

Cruickshank's hands fluttered upon his person, but couldn't find what he was looking for. His eyes never left the water.

Out there?

Bootleggers

Gotta pair 'a low boots if ya want 'em. There in the shanty. Would hate t' burnish the polish on them leather shoes.

Allie heaved once and the skiff slid easily off the beach. He waited, as Cruickshank stepped unbalanced into it. The harbor had wind and waves and Allie rowed against the tide. Cruickshank held tight to each side of the keel and talked to keep his mind off the short row.

Never took to the water. But I gotta say, 'is some system ye got out here.

Works alright I'd say. These past few years.

The way things are? Nowadays? It's hard, son. More motors on the road. More boats in the water.

It's the salt. The way we got it here? It's all about the salt.

Cruickshank stuck his cap onto his knee so it wouldn't be lost overboard. One hand let go of the keel only long enough for Cruickshank to toss the cigarette end from his mouth.

I know. I can feel it on my skin the whole ride back.

The skiff slid broadside to the vessel and as Allie pulled the oars Cruickshank stood and grabbed frantically to her hull. Both tipped up and down on the waves. The skiff was less steady than the bigger vessel which was ballast with a stack of wooden crates, each filled with the fine product that people like Cruickshank drove such distances for.

Allie tied up the bow of the skiff.

G' on up now, I'll tie the stern.

Cruickshank climbed up hurried and clumsy, and his legs kicked like a child to find purchase from one vessel to the other. His eyes adjusted to the darkness over the water and he smiled when he saw the wooden crates, stacked and sodden—still—after being submerged.

Once aboard, Allie stood next to him.

If the red maple leaf says true I'd say it's mostly that Canadian rye. Some o' that sugar cane rum, too—though as to what kind I ain't so sure 'cause o' the glass, but I'd say it's that dark stuff up from the Caribbean. Those tins there are that Belgian alcohol: ye know, stuff tastes kinda like soapy old potatoes. Knock the top o' yer friggin' head off.

Cruickshank counted each with a pointed finger.

And none of 'em broken?

None, s'far as I can tell. They set 'em on good sandy bottom.

Jesus. Good. Goodgoodgood. All of it.

Allie dropped back into the skiff and Cruickshank hefted the cases and handed them down as Allie stacked the first of them mid-ship for ballast. The cases were half-stacked off the vessel when Cruickshank paused to arch his back. He turned and looked to the half-moon, which was orange-yellow in the east.

That a radio station? There on the beach?

Nope. That's Old Harbor Station.

Bootleggers

What kind o' station is it then?

Life saving station. U.S. Coast Guard.

Cruickshank looked to the small man below him in the dory. Hesitancy crept into his posture.

That building's federal?

Mister don't you worry none. Gave the captain o' that station there a ride back to East Orleans just last week, so he could get back down the beach. This night he don't give a care what we do.

Allie took his place between the crates in the stern of the skiff and sculled them back towards Scatteree with a single oar. Cruickshank sat easy atop two crates, with his back against the others and his elbows up behind him. His legs were outstretched over the four tins and he wagged his feet—the right over the left—to some passage or tune that played in his head. The skiff set low the short trip ashore and maybe twice the waves splashed over the side against the crates, but Cruickshank didn't give a thought or motion to keeping his feet dry.

Y'know it's easy to get here. One road in and out. Yer here, right off of it.

Cruickshank had never seen such country: the sparse mixture of water and earth, low country with few trees, and hilltops in which to view the long horizon across the shore to the harbor. Then, the stretch of the barrier beach and the ocean, all the way to Europe.

And at the beginning this quiet shore where they met.

Kinda the worn edge of the world out here.

Yuh. You n' I'll never see the day, but someday that whole beach'll go. Ocean'll take it.

Both the city men and Allie's company watched them reach the beach, unmoving, like spectators at some crucial event.

These crates belong to us while they're on the water. Soon as they get on land, they're yours.

Allie stood up.

They ain't on land. Not yet.

Cruickshank went from the skiff, across the beach, and the driver of the vehicle procured an envelope, heavy and unsealed. Allie stepped out of the dory as Cruickshank returned to the shore, and the deal was struck.

Back her right down an' we'll load ye up. Then you boys can leave.

From the journal of Eva Parks (Griffin) Watts

Sun 11 Feb 34

22 above this AM and stayed up and above that all day. Quite a nice day and Ma, Willie, & I took a ride in PM to So Orleans to see Bay which was frozen over all the way to No Beach over by the islands. Back to Ida's for a while. Ed Long came for Sarah to go for a ride. Home & had lunch & down to Allie's in eve. & sat around open fire.

Tues 13 Feb 34

Cloudy and light snow with temp 30.

In PM Ida and I went to Evelyn Jones' to plan for Eastern Star Entertainment. Grew suddenly colder in PM and at bedtime down to 12 above.

Wed 14 Feb 34

Temp 4 above, clear and sunny. A strong NW wind. Allie & Eliz. & Dick up to dinner to help us eat a nice fresh fish. Making a coat for Dicky out of an old one of Ma's. Ida, Sarah, and Phil down for a little while in eve. Men went to shellfish meeting at Board of Trade. Nearly froze as no fire there. Saw Sarah's bed for her little home on the beach. 10 above at 11:30 PM.

6th of May 1937

Father was on the water that morning early, but he had told his sons in bed the night before that if they wanted a chance to see the airship, they would have to spend the day watching the sky.

Dicky wanted eggs for breakfast but wee Arlen was sick and his mother hadn't the time. His cereal bowl was half-full of Maypo, which tasted like wet paper and made worse as it cooled. He hadn't stirred in the dollop of honey like Mother told him to, and all the sweetness was gone in two and a half mouthfuls. He didn't dare sneak another dollop from the round jar in the pantry, for Mother was very good at remembering how things were once she left the room.

The cool kitchen was made warm by the stove. Worse than the taste of the Maypo was the smell of the onion syrup, which simmered that morning on the stove and permeated every room in the house like a low fog. The onion syrup was Mother's cure for all their provincial ailments: everything from fever to foul language. Dicky had been force-fed it more than once and he knew how bad it would be for his young brother, who was small and sick and would cry in disgust at the taste of it. His father said it smelled so bad it would gag a maggot.

Emery finished his Maypo quickly—with salt, even!—and he drank down his glass of milk as Eliz. walked into the kitchen from Arlen's bedside. She pinched the two brothers by their collars and tugged them up and out of their chairs. Her fingers were very strong; she'd rip the hair from their heads if she ever got angry.

Out! Out now while yer brother's sick!

Emery was big enough to squirm out of her grip but Dicky was small and thin and helpless and she led him towards the kitchen door like a poorly trained pet and didn't let go until he was halfway through it. She turned towards the stove and took up the large kettle that set next to the onion syrup, and with both hands and held it out to Emery, who sullenly tried to sneak past.

Ye take this to Mr. Baker at the post office. And it's warm, so don't be spillin' it. And take yer brother with ye.

Emery walked restlessly with the kettle, despite the post office being only a few houses north up the Stony Hill Road. He was four years older than Dicky and seemed mindful of keeping his little brother behind him on their walk. Dicky knew why Emery had his moods. Wayne had gone back to Tabor Academy again, and Emery missed him. Dicky realized there were some times when Emery liked being a younger brother, too.

6th of May 1937

The air smelled green with cut grass and across Old Harbor Road Uncle Joe and Aunt Ida's field was freshly mowed and ready for baseball. The grass looked damp and if the brothers walked through it barefoot the grass would stick to their feet and ankles and wouldn't fall off until the sun warmed them. The old burgundy door to the post office was half-open and Emery walked through with the kettle as Dicky stopped just inside to pat Maggie, the dog, who was too lazy and too old to wander much past the threshold. She was old and crippled like her master and she lay by the doorway and itched herself for most of the day. Sometimes she'd scratch and an elusive woodtick would fly from behind her ear and burst against the lower half of the post office wall, an area dotted maroon with the remnants of her previous infestations. She wasn't young and she wasn't clean in the least, but she was a good dog and her tail wagged well enough when Dicky patted her head.

Emery walked with the chowder along the counter and towards the back-office room where the mail was sorted.

Hi! Mr. Baker!

Postmaster Harry Baker slid himself from behind the plaid curtain that separated the front of the office from the rear. He was crippled from childhood polio, but he had a chair fastened to wooden rails along the floor, and he slid near to everywhere inside the office unhindered. He tipped his head back and looked down at Emery from behind crooked eyeglasses set low on his nose.

What is it? You. And you? Allie's boys. What is it?

Brotcha some chowder. Dad made it last night and Mom wants you ta have it.

Harry inspected the kettle closely.

Oooooo.

The kettle was warm and more than half-full of chowder and smelled wonderfully of milk and clams and onions heavily laced with salt pork.

Mmmmm. Right. In here then.

Behind the plaid curtain Harry's table was cluttered with stacks of newspapers, simple instruments of weights and measures, many overflowing ashtrays, and all sorts of boxes, cases and envelopes just arrived or bound for somewhere else. He cleared a spot for the kettle and Emery set it down. Then Harry procured his Bugler, his papers and his rolling machine and placed them at the corner of the table. He pointed—with something of both a grimace and a grin as he bit down on his empty cigarette holder—and Emery sat.

Don't 'cha roll 'em too tight either goddammit or ye'll do 'em over.

It was a legitimate threat. Emery had spent most of one past summer afternoon re-rolling a dozen of Harry Baker's cigarettes.

Dicky's laughter came through the plaid curtain and Harry swiped it aside and rolled back to the front, where Maggie

6th of May 1937

licked the small boys hand as if she hadn't tasted anything so good in years.

Mr. Baker can I go fer a walk with her?

Harry motioned the boy towards him with an unassuming tilt of his hand.

Sure, why don't ya. Somethin'll come out of her I'm sure, one end or t'other. Put my feet up for me will ya?

Mr. Baker's legs were disproportionately scrawny and his feet were bent at different angles, and it was difficult for him to reach down and set them up comfortably.

Tie up m' laces too.

Dicky took the time to tie them good and tight and then he was out the door with Maggie, who led him at a decent pace along Scatteree Road with her tongue out and her tail moving side-to-side due either to sheer pleasure or a bad hip. She stopped to sniff about the salt pond which was calm and dark and free of the green scum that covered the surface in summer, and there were red-wing blackbirds in the reeds surrounding it.

Konk-a-reeeeeeeee.

Dicky thought about walking to the end of the road and to the shanties, but he knew his father was out on the ocean fishing for halibut, and that he wasn't to be around the shanties without his father being there. Uncle Joe had a shanty right next to his father's, but he wasn't to bother Uncle Joe either.

He was Dicky's favorite person in all the world, with his floppy hat and his pipe and his wide face and his laughter. He and Father got on well, which Mother said was fortunate—Uncle Joe being married to father's sister Ida—and they laughed a lot when they were together. If there was anyone about, they laughed along with them, even Mother, who didn't always smile when they spoke together in their way in front of the children.

The boy and the dog turned onto Old Wharf Road. It was a steady incline and Maggie walked in short steps and was a long time up it. At the crest of the hill Dicky saw someone in the yard of the Old Harbor Inn, dressed in a white t-shirt. He saw that it was not old Rufus Nickerson, but he wasn't sure which Williard it was because both of them wore white t-shirts. Whoever it was walked behind a mower and there were soggy blades of grass piled up in neat rows on the lawn. Dicky heard the mower from far away.

Clipclipclipclipclipclipclipclipclipclipclipclip.

He saw most of the harbor from the hill: every mooring was vacant and he saw the ocean all the way to the horizon for many miles. There was neither a boat nor bird to be seen. In a month or so there would be sailboats moored alongside fishing vessels, and the harbor would be dotted with hulls of all colors, and sails like bright flags. On the Fourth there would be catboat races and a lot of folks from town would be there. Anne and Crosby Lincoln would be there, both blonde and tan in pretty white sundresses.

6th of May 1937

Herbert Baker had a workshop where Old Wharf Road bent at a right angle and there was the clatter of steel and machinery from within. A light smoke almost like steam rose out of a flue through the roof. Mr. Baker was a machinist and a strong purveyor of Haig & Haig Five-Star whiskey. Dicky knew if he took the time to look he'd find forgotten empty bottles of it strewn about the property. On days when he and his brothers were particularly bored, they'd venture down the hill and spend the afternoon smashing the bottles against the cement foundation of his workshop. Mother disapproved heatedly when she found out, but Mr. Baker didn't seem to mind.

Across from Herbert Baker's Dicky saw Bobby Long in the motions of mowing his parent's front lawn in an over-sized t-shirt and dungarees. Bobby was a year younger than Dicky, and they got along best because Bobby only had a younger sister, and Dicky didn't play much at all with Arlen—him only three—and Wayne and Emery didn't play with Dicky much unless there was a baseball game. He and Bobby were nearly inseparable in summer; Father called them the Lone Ranger and Tonto.

Heya Bobby!

Bobby Long stopped mowing and rubbed his grimy hands on his grimier shirt. The grass was damp with dew and heavy, and there were a few sprigs of it in Bobby's hair and Dicky wondered for a second how it got there. Bobby's pantcuffs were wet and his old shoes were green. If Dicky had mowed the lawn, he would have mowed barefoot.

Heya Dicky.

Still in deep with yer folks?

Yuh. Ma says I'll prob'ly be doin' chores 'til Rapture.

Oh yeah? When's that?

I dunno. I'm hopin' before school lets out.

It was almost two weeks ago when the two boys built their first campfire of the season in one of the open fields along Old Harbor Road, when the lovely warm wind from the new May came suddenly and strong from the south, and in less than a minute turned the high grasses of the Cow Yard into half an acre of smoke and flame. It was astonishing, the speed at which the fire spread, and both boys knew quickly there was no respite from the damage, and panicked and turned a full sprint for home. Fortunately that day George Goodspeed had driven up from the Boulevard and saw the smoke, and Dicky heard the bells of the firetruck from his favorite hiding place. He endured a few days of the rosary, reconciliation and the lash, but truly Dicky loved to pray with his mother, so other than wearing a welt on his rear end from his father's belt for near two days, he figured he got off easy.

Bobby looked uneasily over his shoulder.

Ma'll get cross if she sees me talkin' to ye. I should get mowin'.

Dicky understood. Mrs. Long was outside all the time and working along her clothesline. If she came out now Dicky would probably be shouted at and shoo-ed away for the second time that morning.

The boy and the dog turned onto Old Harbor Road. Bertha Armington's dog Junior barked from the rear yard of her white cottage, and the frequency increased to a constant as they passed. Maggie stopped—half-hearing—and she looked side to side with her clouded vision, but nothing could be seen amoung the unmown grass. She responded, though, enthusiastically and without breath.

Huff. Huff.

Then Mrs. Armington began to scold her from the back door, so you couldn't see her either. Mrs. Armington was a nice old woman, and rich, although father insisted she was not singing from the same hymn sheet as everyone else. Most of her teeth were missing and if you got close enough you could see the white whiskers sprouting from her chin. Her voice was harsh and cracked. Father was right: she sounded like a screech owl.

Hush! You hush! Hush!

Dicky stopped walking at the Cow Yard, which set to the east at the base of Thayer's Hill. He hadn't a clue why they called it that. Freeman Phillip's old man had a farm, and so did old Freddie P. Allen near Ryder's Cove, and almost everyone in Old Harbor had a henhouse and garden, but as far as he knew there had never been cows in the Cow Yard. The field was still flattened and burnt but there were short strands of grass growing anew that looked very green in the sun against all that fading black. Maggie put her snout in the air and sniffed but there were no rabbits there to chase, only charcoal.

The young boy and the old dog turned back towards the office and her place on the floor. They passed the old homestead and the faint notes of *Elvira Madigan* floated from the open window and over the road. Mother played it often when her family was sick. She must have believed that it was Mozart who wrote music to cure the young and the sick.

The Rose Cottage sat on the corner of Old Harbor Road and was yet in bloom. The Geary's had not arrived yet for the summer season, but by June the house on the corner blossomed pink roses on all of its sides and trellises and intertwined along the fenceline. From the top of Thayer's Hill you could see the house in summer: a burst of bright color among the fields and the scattered white houses. The Geary's were from New York, and fine people.

Then Maggie caught a scent of something or other and her arthritic shuffle must have eased a bit for she moved quickly past Mr. Baker's post office and down the Stony Hill Road and squatted near the steps of the Guild Hall and relieved herself in a weak stream. The road weaved downward; to the east the land rose up to a great hill covered in pine trees, then fell quite steeply downward to the shore. Dicky never wandered up into Old Harbor Pines alone. It was always dark under the trees even in the daylight, and at night the owls sounded out from the darkest places. Father said there was a hermit living in some kind of shed half-built atop the hill, where he lived alone, dirty and bearded. Sometimes this hermit could be seen digging for clams along the far shoreline but he possessed great cunning, and no one ever got a good look at him because he'd always see you first and would disappear quickly into the dark of Old Harbor Pines.

They finished their walk and returned. Emery had finished his cigarette rolling. A dozen had come out quite decent. Mr. Baker busied himself with the scant morning mail.

Go ahead now. Take one of somethin' from behind the counter. One, now.

Each brother walked out the post office door with a yard-length of black licorice. Emery chewed on his greedily. Dicky twirled his around in front of him like a shield as he walked, and bit down on his lower lip as if such a thing took great concentration.

The airship came over the treetops suddenly from the north and if they hadn't known it was coming, they might have been shaken by the enormity of it, it seeming to take up half the morning sky and the daylight with it. They saw the shadow of it on the dirt road and they sprinted the short way to home, through the front door and up the stairs to their attic bedroom where the windows faced east and over the water.

Wee Arlen's face had an ill sheen of sweat and snot and his light hair was slick atop the near perfect sphere of his head. He looked very small alone on the bed resting half-sitting up among many pillows. Emery helped him out from under the layer of blankets and to the window so he could see as far as his older brothers. He held onto Emery as tight as he could; he breathed heavy and there was a heat to him as his body fought against its illness. Arlen looked to where his big brother pointed out the window.

It was bigger than any tree or vessel or building in town, and it came over the trees and low above the house, a great silver wonder against the blue sky and none of it in shadow. Dicky saw a woman in white seated in the lower cabin and the pattern of her porcelain teacup looked pink. Emery saw a man in a black coat and white shirt leaning with his hands on the sill of the cabin windows and the sunlight reflecting off his pocket watch like a dull coin. The silhouette of porters marched back and forth behind them.

Arlen saw his first great wonder of man.

The brothers waved their hands absently, but no one saw the three boys in the window with their mouths open, for no one waved back.

The airship's rudder bore the red flag with the black crooked X that Dicky saw in the newspaper recently. The gothic letters of its name seemed fifty-feet high, and the scarlet script of each letter was brilliant in the morning daylight.

HINDENBURG

6th of May 1937

Dicky couldn't quite sound it out.

What's it say?

Emery told him. Dicky had never heard such a thing.

What's it mean?

It don't mean nothin'. It's just a name.

They watched the airship turn and dip and point itself southward. It followed the way of the shoreline, then passed out of sight forever.

From the journal of Eva Parks (Griffin) Watts

Fri Mar 1 1934

A lovely day. Almost calm and temp 32 at 8:30 AM. Harbor full of ice and large pieces 6 and 8 ft. thick stuck on flat. At noon temp 50. Ma, Ida, & I went to Helen Eldredge's to a Star Cycle tea in PM. Others present Reb Ryder, Florence Eldredge. A pleasant afternoon. Reb spilled tea in her lap.

At bedtime temp 34.

Sat Mar 2 1934

Temp 40 with a rain, & also fog. Rain stopped in AM but fog continued. Made doughnuts cleaned up downstairs. Ma & I sewing in PM. She on the cross stitch runner & me on patchwork quilt--in eve., stayed at Allie's for he and Eliz. to go up to Hall as their bowling club had gentlemen's night. Fog and rain all night.

Sun Mar 3 1934

Another foggy calm day and temp 40 in AM & up to 50 in middle of day. Foggy all day. Capt. Wescott of Old Harbor C.G. came this PM to bid us goodbye, as he leaves in the morning for his home in North Carolina, as he is transferring to that district. A fine man & we shall miss him greatly at camp. He was so good to us.

A Day's Pay

Offshore was humid and there was no wind, and the haze over the ocean hid most of the glare from the sun. Inside the pilot house the summer air was unmoving and smelled like old salt and motor oil, and because it was hard to breathe on such days, Allie chewed on the bit of his pipe unlit the entire way to the fishgrounds.

It was worse to be on land with the bugs and the chaff of the unmowed fields and the intolerable greenheads by the shore, which-- since the full moon passed recently--wouldn't perish en masse until August.

It was July and the ocean was full of fish. The ice had come into the harbor in January, and Allie had no work off the water, but the ice broke in March and there were haddock, and by mid-May the lobster pots were set and the halibut in from the deep water.

Bill Speight stood in the stern near the barrels and dipped his hands into the ocean to dampen the lines. His hands stayed wet so he kept his head turned to keep his cigarette lit. He worked with his eyes closed and his face towards the sun. Bill was a distant cousin to Allie, and lived further east down the

Stony Hill Road in a small house with a big yard on the corner of Cotchpinicut Road.

Allie's two sons were there on the vessel that day to work, to stay quiet, and to learn to catch the mackerel. They went to task on the chum--which smelled unholy if it sat on the boat for a time and got hot in the sun--but they didn't mind the smell if they were allowed to fish with their father. Emery held the frozen foot-long English herring into the grinder while young Dicky turned the handle. They both used both hands because both were small and the herring were frozen. Dicky pressed his lips together tight and sweat darkened the blonde hair about his forehead. The brothers filled half of a ten-quart pail with a mix of the fish grind and sea water. If the ocean was rough, or the current ran especially strong, they'd add oatmeal to thicken it.

The surface of the ocean was calm and green and despite the haze Allie saw a good distance to the east where the mackerel schooled: thousands of them, about a half-mile off the beach. Allie brought the *Virginia* slow up on the school, which rippled like small circles of wind on the water. The green ocean underneath the vessel turned black with fish.

Start the chum boys. Toss it far out, now.

The boys scooped the chum overboard with long dirty white ladles and it spread in an oily slick to the fore and aft.

Dad! Lookit 'em! They're right below us! Dad! The whole school of 'em! Em'ry lookit 'em! Lookit 'em!

A Day's Pay

Allie cut the motor.

Keep workin' the chum, now. They'll come up.

The boys worked the chum; they leaned over the port rail and watched the bits of ground herring sink down into the dark swimming tangle of shadow far below. The mackerel wouldn't bite if they were schooling; jigs and tackle and specialty methods were all equally useless.

The chum worked like it always did: slowly at first, then all at once the mackerel rose and their fins and tails turned the greasy ocean top into drops of froth and mist. In the heat and the haze the salt spray made rainbows.

Go boys! Don't stop tossin 'til that barrel's full!

The boys had their lines ready and baited and they knew where they were and they knew how to fish, but at first they were excited and clumsy because each wanted to catch more fish than the other, even though Emery always did because he was older and could haul his handline quicker. Their very first tosses were poorly executed.

Don't cross yer jigs! And don't catch yer brother in the ear!

Bill Speight stood furthest aft. He had a pair of gangens at the end of his line and each lead-head jig he baited with a piece of white fish belly about the size of his fingernail. The gangens spun in two circles as Bill cast the line out in a great arc to the far side of the school. When the fish were on full, he and Allie tossed and hauled and slatted the fish in one smooth motion. The bottom of each barrel between them was lined with block ice and ocean water and the mackerel went in fresh out of the ocean: brilliant silver, blue, green and striped with black, twenty inches of perfection they were, and each nearly identical to the next. They went into the barrel and twisted and flipped for a few seconds inside, then lay straight and stiffened.

Dicky didn't know of a better place in the world to be than with the fish and the laughing gulls appearing overhead and the heat from the sun and saltiness in the air. The fishing was easy—they needn't wait for a strike—and Dicky knew that father would give both him and his brother each a quarter if they behaved well and worked hard and stood where he told them to on the boat. Dicky loved baseball, too, and he figured mackerel fishing was akin to throwing the baseball with his father in his Aunt Ida's field across the street from the old homestead, in the late light of the summer before Mother called him in for the night. He loved baseball, but he never got a cent for a game of catch.

The second barrel was nearly full when Bill--furthest aft--stopped suddenly and pointed, and Allie cursed and tossed his jig backhanded onto the deck.

Son of a bitch. Boys... hold yer lines.

The boys held their lines. They stepped back from the rail and peered sternwards to where Bill was pointing, towards the sharp grey dorsal fin of a shark breaking near three feet out of the water. The ocean swirled behind a tail that swept slowly, deliberately side-to-side against the slow current.

There were sharks everywhere in the water, always: blue sharks were a numerous nuisance and horribly aggressive; worse they were poisonous and inedible, so without a market were killed and left to sink to the ocean floor. Thresher sharks—called swingtails—hadn't the size or demeanor of the blues, and often their awkward long tails got tangled up in the trawl. There were great whites in the deep water—near the Figs, some forty miles south-southeast of the harbor—and those would cut the gear entirely from the bottom: one thousand feet of groundline, with hooks and bait every six feet, gear, fish, everything, lost. They followed the fish up the coast from the south in August when the sun was out and strong and the currents held their temperatures from the long summer. Big and bulbous and vicious characters. No one dared untangle one alive. At the surface, a single slug from a shotgun to the back of its head worked best. Like the blues they were poisonous and would sink, useless, to the bottom.

The shark swam close and the four fishermen watched the quick splash of mackerel disperse in all directions and disappear. A circle of foam collected briefly on the surface. The fish were gone, the gulls flew off, and it was suddenly quiet without the sound of the birds and the vessel at drift.

They had only filled a single barrel.

There was only the shark and the *Virginia*, which was thirty-eight feet long. Under the water the shark looked almost half that.

Em'ry you and yer brother get over t' the barrels. Keep from the rail.

Allie put his foot atop the starboard rail and watched the shark swim back and forth across the port side of his vessel: it was forever in motion, a deep grey, and it would have been difficult to see if not for the sleek triangle of its dorsal fin. It half-circled once and when it turned from the scent of the fish Allie saw the stark white of its underside flash suddenly. It swam at them head on, revealing two jagged rows of teeth along its lower jaw.

Bill leaned over the rail. He looked at his cousin and smiled. His small eyes were wide and white and set close together. Both his teeth and moustache were equally crooked.

Allie that's a Mako. He'd be worth some money wouldn't ye say? If... if we could land 'em.

Allie stood still with his foot on the rail and crossed his arms and was quiet. He wore an irritated look and his jaws worked as he ground his teeth together because he had no pipe bit to chew on.

Bill, get the iron.

Bill sprung to the pilot house where the swordfish iron hung within arms reach from nearly anywhere. Allie started coiling quite a few fathoms of rope through his fingers so that it lay in large easy loops on the deck.

The boys stood by the empty barrels, and kept from the rail.

Em'ry, hook the jigs over the rail.

Emery hung the jig-lines over the port rail to clear the deck of hooks. His father took the swordfish iron in his hands.

Clear these coils from the others. Set 'em off the deck.

Allie was prepared to stand by for a time by the rail, with the iron high near his ear, ready for when the shark came close, or if it would at all. He was consigned to the situation that the mackerel would not return, but aware that his cousin was correct, and there may be a market for the fish, since there wasn't a single man's pay aboard the vessel as they were. But the shark made it easy, and turned across the bow and along the starboard gunwale, turned again at the stern and when it made to turn again the iron was high at Allie's ear. He struck the shark quick like a learned harpooner, and the heavy dart punched through the back of its gills, held, and detached from the shaft. The blood was immediate and bloomed in a cloudy red fan that spread quickly like a scarlet stormcloud in the turn of the tide. The shark shook violently, and the bloody ocean water sprayed both men. Bill spat out what fell into his open mouth. With two great sweeps of its tail the shark made straight for the bottom and sixty fathoms worth of rope uncoiled rapidly behind it.

Dicky stood behind his brother, not moving once from the barrels. He was not certain and not at all in agreement on the motion of landing the shark, with its imposture and all its teeth which didn't belong on board but belonged to such a monster deep beneath the ocean, and not on the surface chasing away all their mackerel. He took a second to think and he knew his father's boat was well-built and safe; he could hide down in the trunk cabin if the shark got away from them. The cockpit was water tight, so he could hide there as well if he needed to.

The shark was mighty strong. The stern-line was taut downwards and the shark kept a steady heading to the south and deep water. The transom dipped downward and creased the slow-rolling calm of the ocean surface with a backward wake, and sometimes the rope would move a few degrees in one direction than another, and it took nearly two hours for the rope to slacken. Allie started the motor, checked his compass, and looked out over the ocean in every direction.

Bill followed him halfway to the pilot house.

Allie, whaddya think?

Allie was sure of his bearings.

I'd say he's towed us nearly two miles.

Shouldn't we keep her at a drift? What if he runs again.

He's made his last run.

A Day's Pay

Bill stood at the helm; Allie moved back to the stern and took up the rope. His face was still grim and hadn't changed much at all with the shark.

Em'ry stand behind me. Coil up that rope he's givin'. Ye watch yer fingers.

Allie pulled with a gentle strength and Emery coiled the taken rope into a large circle atop the cedar planks of the deck. It all went slow: Allie gave the shark rope when it wanted to run, and hauled again and gave back, for a long while and no one spoke. After twenty minutes Allie had sweat through every piece of clothing save his low boots. The sweat on the brown skin of his neck didn't cool him: the air over the water was saturating, and he worked slowly as if under the water with the fish.

Bill take him for a bit, will ye?

Bill clambered out of the pilot house and took the rope eagerly and hauled awkwardly as if he were drunk, and trying to dance. His tongue poked out the side of his mouth. The shark tugged three times hard and Bill had to brace himself suddenly with a foot upon the transom to keep from being brought overboard. It wasn't Bill's way to give up. Allie figured if he ever held on and went over, he might not have the sense to let go until he were a few fathoms down.

Dammit, Bill, ye let 'em go! Let 'em go if he runs! Em'ry don't grab that rope lest it's given to ye.

Dicky watched everyone around him; he knew why his father yelled like he did. He knew at all times to mind his hands and his fingers because they got slicked-up and slippery from the fish, and if you weren't wearing gloves and caught something with any size to it the rope would pass through your palms and fingers and take any and all skin away with it. Neither of the boys had hands like their father. Sometimes a line would run on him, too, but nothing ever seemed to hurt his hands.

Allie took the rope up again at the end, and the shark came to the surface as the last of its strength and lifeblood seeped out of the wound in its gills like listless trails of smoke. Allie had struck it deep. The shark made one final surge, but Allie didn't let him run. Soon it lay distal on the surface and didn't move.

It was quiet and the ocean was red. Allie looked to his sons and nodded.

Come on now boys. Let's get 'em aboard.

The boys took quick steps to their father and held the rope where he told them to. They pulled, and the father urged them on and they pulled harder. Bill Speight made a quick loop with a second rope and lashed it around the tail of the shark. It took four attempts to haul it upwards out of the ocean, for the shark was heavy and long and awkward, with most of its weight through its middle. They struggled to bring that weight broadside into the boat.

A Day's Pay

Watch it's yap. Stay clear o' the head.

The got the shark rolled onto its back and it lay unmoving on the starboard rail.

Back boys. Get back now.

The shark rolled again, and they all backed away quick as it fell with an exhausted thud onto the deck.

Dicky felt a bit unnerved at first: with the shark so close there on the deck, drowning in the open air. It was striking: one of many beautiful monsters from the deep parts of the ocean. Strong and smooth and dark it was, with an eye staring up at them unblinking and an expression of permanent anger in its eye and jaw.

It shook three times suddenly, and the flat of its tail rocked the deck hard enough that Dicky and his brother might have lost their feet if they weren't still in their place by the barrels. The shark lay on the deck, bled some more and died slowly. Its jaw worked, and there were a few missing teeth from each of its four rows, yet none looked any less sharp, and Dicky knew with a sudden, singular snap the shark would remove a small human limb with a most terrible sound.

It was a short ride home, still, despite being towed for those couple of hours. Allie smoked his pipe and he and Bill passed a pint bottle of Riando dark rum between them. He didn't say a word to the boys, but Dicky knew he was happy, and Dicky was happy too because he never thought his father could catch a shark with his hands and that was saying something even if his father didn't get what he wanted for it.

When they brought it ashore and Jot Ryder first saw the shark, he laughed.

What in God's name have ye brought me today, Allie?

Whaddya think? Bill's nearly got 'em cleaned out. Think there'd be a market for 'em?

Jot laughed again. The herring gulls began to flock and scream around Bill and the blood.

We'll sell 'em. If not in Boston, well, New York'll find a somewhere for it.

Bill finished dressing the shark there on the shore and some of the mackerel seemed still half-alive in its gullet. Jot had his camera and he took a picture with the fishermen and their catch: Allie held the iron and Bill held the shark's mouth open by grabbing its snout with both hands and the boys took a knee to either side. When it was done they each cut out a tooth to wear around the necks for when school started.

One week later Allie got a check from the Berman Fish Company of New York for sixty-four dollars, which was a lot of money for one day, and one fish.

From the journal of Eva Parks (Griffin) Watts

Fri 8 Mar 34

Lovely day & temp 20 at 7 AM rising rapidly to 36 by noon.

Ma feeling better. Eliz. heard last night from home that sister Minnie failing fast. Sara & Ed Long called for a few minutes. Ed on liberty & on way home.

Sat 9 Mar 34

Light South E wind & cloudy & temp around 26. Started to snow middle of day & increased rapidly, wind breezing to NE & by bedtime a good blizzard, worst of winter.

Sun 10 Mar 34

Cloudy with temp 28 & No. wind & air full of snow. Big drifts everywhere and for first time in years road had to be shovelled by hand before plough could get through. Grew colder during day, to 26 at bed time. Minnie Blankenship died at 9 PM after a years illness with TB.

The Guild Hall Supper

It took all morning and most of the afternoon for Dicky to finish his drawing. He held it in both hands as he walked from home next door to the old store on the corner of Old Wharf Road and Old Harbor, where his father, Harold Brett and old Joe Lincoln stood and spoke and laughed. The two wings of Mr. Lincoln's hair were oiled and parted down the middle; he nodded and listened with his short pipe between his teeth and his face up to the sun. A small pencil and notebook were closed in his hands above the ample circumference of his belt. Mr. Lincoln laughed, and the funny waddle of his second chin moved. Dicky couldn't hear the story his father told because his father laughed as he spoke. Mr. Lincoln spoke with Father quite often in the late summer, usually on Mr. Lincoln's son Freeman's back porch, which was also next door, and always with the pipe in his mouth and taking notes on a yellow-papered record book spread open on one knee.

Harold Brett wore a wide-brim hat that shaded his face, and the only feature that struck out from it was an unshaven chin and a cigarette lit in a long holder. It burned in the sun and Dicky knew that Mr. Brett was laughing too because the smoke wiggled upward in wispy S's and his shoulders hitched up and down with his hands in his pockets. Mr. Brett lived off Old Harbor Road in a beautiful big house at the end of a long driveway, before the low-roofed cottages of the Summers', the McKee's, the Wilson's, and the shore. Mr. Brett was an artist, and spent most of his time that summer inside his studio at an easel and indirect sunlight. Dicky saw how pale his cheeks and chin were.   His two sons attended Tabor Academy with Wayne. Mr. Brett and his father were great friends.

Dicky held the drawing in front of him with both hands close to his chest. His mother encouraged him with his artwork; his father was more indifferent to it. He walked straight towards Mr. Brett, who turned to him while smiling.

Whaddya got there, young man?

Dicky handed Mr. Brett his drawing.

Hi.

Mr. Brett cast his eyes over the drawing for a longer amount of time that Dicky ever thought he would.

Watch your proportions. Watch your perspective.

Uhhh—

Harold Brett kept smiling.

Watch your size and distance.

He held the drawing back towards Dicky with two pointed fingers.

The Guild Hall Supper

Keep it up.

Dicky took it with both hands.

Mostly I draw cowboys.

He turned away from Mr. Brett with his head lower than when he first walked over. Back inside the kitchen his mother readied herself for the evening at the Guild Hall. She readied her pot of Boston baked beans on the counter with dishtowels, removed her apron and flattened her freshly ironed summer dress around herself.

Go getcher father for me, dear.

Dicky let his head roll back on his neck, as if it was too heavy for him to hold up.

He's back outside with Mr. Lincoln.

Tell him we're ready to head over. I'm sure Mr. Lincoln will grace us all with his presence later.

Eliz never talked down about anybody, but she didn't seem to get along with old Joe Lincoln as well as his father did.

They walked to Stony Hill Road and to the Guild Hall as a family. Wayne carried the beanpot out in front of him with two plaid towels underneath and Emery walked alongside him. Dicky walked with Arlen who was young and wandered off to everywhere except the short way they were going. He walked with his brother so his parents could walk together, and he and his brother were the last to get there.

Dicky decided there wasn't much reason at all for him to go to the Old Harbor Guild Hall. Surely his mother would ask him to sing on the stage, and he'd tell her he didn't want to, and she'd ask him again anyway, and in the end Dicky didn't want to disappoint his mother because she rarely asked for anything. There wasn't anyone close to his age other than Bobby Long, and he feared having to keep a watch on the young ones, or to sit and be surrounded by the older ladies who would talk at him and not allow him to answer. Father and Uncle Joe called them the hens. And he wasn't allowed around the men when they stood huddled in the south corner of the hall around a punch bowl, which he wasn't allowed to drink from. Dicky didn't see much reason for him to be there at all. His father sometimes walked in and out of doorways backwards, that way—he said—no one would know whether he was coming or going. On the walk Dicky pondered the logic and concluded it might be his only way out. He planned to try it. After dinner.

Bertha Armington was the only person from the neighborhood who drove, and her '24 Buick was parked crooked in the lot, near halfway into the trees of Old Harbor Pines. There was plenty of space in the lot but evidently Bertha couldn't find it. The sound of the neighborhood--and those from the outside as well--came through the open door, with the creak of footsteps on the old floor, and a crowd under high ceilings talking over each other in unison, and the laughter which was constant and held together by the ceiling, floor, and all four walls.

The Guild Hall Supper

Arlen made for the stairs with the stumbling vigor of a toddler in motion. He took the steps one at a time with the help of both hands. Allie followed, crawling up the stairs and through the doorway after his son, with exaggerated movements of his arms and legs. Dicky heard the skid of table legs across the wooden floor and the sudden gay tenor of women's laughter. Aunt Eva was distinct among them: with a humor and laugh much like her brother, she sometimes laughed so hard she turned red, and lost her breath and had to sit.

Harry Mallowes was there behind his truck with the wooden sides backed up near the door of the hall. Dicky saw stacks of sandbags in the rear amongst a few chipped bowling balls and pins. If the children made their own alley lined with the sandbags along the far wall they could bowl by themselves all night for free.

Whaddya say, there, Little Al?

Mr. Mallowes couldn't remember which brother's name belonged to which, now that there were four of them.

Come an' grab some o' these pins.

Thomas Haley was standing inside of the open doorway. Mr. Haley, who lived next door, was held in dear regard by Eliz. and therefore the family, for he drove the family to church in the fall when it was cold and father was out fishing. Dicky enjoyed driving with Mr. Haley because he always drove a red car. Clean and very red, a color he didn't see much of.

He saw that Dicky's arms were full and he patted Dicky once on the shoulder as he walked passed.

There were Fred and Lillian Devlin, and Bert and Hattie, Fred and Bernice, Harry, and Ben who were all Bakers. Some of the Mallowses, who through some relation with Rufus Nickerson, were a distant cousin, and so related to Aunt Ida, who was married to Uncle Joe, who was Rufus' nephew.

Inside the men moved towards the eastern side of the hall, a dozen there already, and there was a hip flask in the pocket of most of their half-circle; they smoked and drank and Dicky knew better to approach them when they met together apart from their homes as fathers and men. In fact, Allie had Wayne, Emery, Bobby Long, Sonny Mallowes and Billy Wescott in a line in front of him. Billy's father had gone away some time ago, as had Eddie Proudfoot's, Dick Haskin's, and Gene and Walter Love's father. They all left the same year. Dicky never met Billy's father, and Billy didn't remember much about him. No one knew where the men went, so no one ever spoke about them. Billy's mother doted on him and his sister Ida with great concern. She didn't work much, or have family. They lived on Cranberry Lane without electricity or water. Their mother was nervous, and Dicky felt bad for her too. Dicky looked about and saw she wasn't near.

And all you boys: ye keep it down to a dull roar inside. No goin' in the rafters n' spittin' in the soup like last time. And-

The Guild Hall Supper

Dicky had only a second to listen before there was a grasp and a tug around his poorly formed bicep, and he was pulled into the turbulence of the crowd.

Cordelia Atwood led him through a maze of women standing mostly in pairs and talking at once, nearer to the stage and the long stretch of tables with similar shaped dishes of different foods, the smallest children encircling the feast. She led and stood Dicky before a great wooden trunk, opened and tall enough that he could not see everything inside of it. Cordelia turned and held her hands together, as if pondering a plan that had begun to work towards a desired result.

Percy and Cordelia Atwood produced some of the minstrel shows in town. They were busy people, well-liked by all, and came a good distance from home to the Guild Hall because of the stage and the piano, and because there were folks like his parents and Uncle Joe who liked to eat and drink with a crowd. They had the triune fortune of wit and voice and strong musical ability.

Now I have it all here! For you and yer brother. Just like last year...

Uhh, Ms. Atwood—

Cordelia moved her hands a lot when she spoke, even when her back was turned.

Take it now so ye'll have it all ready.

The top half of her bore into the maw of the open trunk and her rear end moved to a few inches from Dicky's eyeballs, he standing close behind her where she had put him, and he arched his back away from her bony derriere and the flowered dress that covered it. He leaned backward and got his face a good foot away without having to move his feet.

Mrs. Atwood--

…just hold out yer arms.

Dicky straightened himself and let his head roll back as he did, and he almost *Awwwwwwwww*-ed but he couldn't be rude to Mrs. Atwood, who was such a nice lady. His arms were already held out with the three wooden bowling pins that crossed them. She hung two raincoats across his twiggy forearms and placed the two umbrellas gently in the crook of his elbows, atop the pins.

One each for you and yer brother…

Um, Ms. Atwood, I don't know if—

…you two are just wonderful! You'll do it just like you did last year…

Dicky might have mumbled some weak refute but then Mrs. Atwood put her hands to either side of his face. There was a gentility to the smooth skin on her palms and fingers that kept his jaw from moving.

Just like you did last year. You and yer brother.

The Guild Hall Supper

Then Mrs. Atwood turned her back, closed the trunk, and walked in the direction of the piano with her arms moving again.

Dicky cleared himself of the crowd of womenfolk before he felt the grip of a hard hand atop his head. He writhed his way out of the grip to see who owned it, and it was his uncle Joe Nickerson who was his favorite other person to be around with his tittering laugh like a birdcall that made everyone else laugh if they heard it, especially at a distance.

Looks like yer all set! Eh?

Dicky looked downward but because of the umbrellas and the jackets and the bowling pins he couldn't stare down at his feet. He shrugged and felt weak with Uncle Joe's hand back atop his skull, and when he spoke the words were mushed together and that felt weak too.

Uh, I dunno, maybe…

Whaddya mean? Get on up there like ye always do.

I dunno. I don't really wanna…

Whaddya mean ye don't wanna? Yer old man an' I are up on that stage damn near half the night!

It was true. His father and Uncle Joe put on little acts for the crowd, and made themselves up to look like the two colored fellows on Mother's packet of Gold Dust Washing Powder.

Uncle Joe moved his hand from Dicky's head to where his neck met his shoulder and he pressed hard with his thumb. There was a second of sinister discomfort and Dicky thought of a mother cat moving her kittens by the nape of their necks, and he hoped Uncle Joe would spare him the embarrassment, and keep him earthbound.

Ye do it for yer mother, eh? She prob'ly don't ask ye for nothin'.

Dicky didn't look at his uncle. He looked downward and sideways and saw his mother start in on the old untuned piano that--though covered to keep the dust off--looked as if it had sat out all night in a rainstorm. Recently his father had mentioned his mother was 'in a way', but he hadn't quite figured out what way that was. His aunts and a few other women fawned over Eliz. as she sat, played a few scales, and smiled as she took requests from the chirping ladies around her. Some in the hall quieted at the sound of music.

After her morning prayers and breakfast Eliz. would be at her Poole piano. She played always, as devout to her music as she was to her missal. There were days after school when Dicky walked into the house and his Aunt Eva or his Aunt Ida or both would mime for him to be quiet as he entered, so as not to disturb the music. She played the organ for the silent movies at the Chatham Theater on Main Street before she had children. On Saturdays she played the vigil mass at Holy Redeemer, and both masses on Sundays. Sacred music was most dear to her, but it was solemn, somewhat private music. At the Guild Hall she played the stride piano, so she began the

The Guild Hall Supper

evening with a few of her favorites: 'Kitten on the Keys' into 'Maple Leaf Rag'.

Uncle Joe chuckled once around the pipe in his mouth and clapped his hands, once.

I tell ya Dicky if I wasn't ta know, you'd think i' twas Scott Joplin.

Dicky didn't know Scott Joplin; perhaps he had come with someone from outside Old Harbor, and he hadn't introduced himself yet. He had no words for Uncle Joe, and Uncle Joe didn't wait for any as he walked away towards the music.

Dicky dragged his feet towards the tables with all the food: his mother's baked beans and Aunt Eva's finnan haddie with the cod that Allie brought to her. One year past Dicky had eaten so much of it that he got sick, quickly. He'd been woken from sleep because of it, and threw up all over his blankets and brothers. On the floor by the table were wood baskets of shellfish, and there were lobsters atop the blocks of ice Elmer Kendrick brought from his icehouse. Freeman Phillips brought over corn from his farm, enough corn for everybody and more, so much it was piled and spilled around a five-gallon pot of fish chowder steaming in the center.

When Anne Lincoln walked through the open door, the sun shone through onto her skin, her summer dress, and her hair, which were amber, pale and golden. She saw him and smiled, but Dicky hadn't the sense enough to smile back. His mouth was unhinged and open, and his heart suddenly felt heavy; his chest swelled and clenched, and for a moment he forgot how to breathe. His stomach dropped down onto the rest of his insides and he put one foot over the other to lock the sudden pressure within his bladder.

Anne's younger sister Crosby popped up next to Dicky's shoulder, and like her sister she was tan and blonde. Dicky's backbone was so that he ended up bent over and looking sideways at her, the way a dog would if they were a good dog. The jackets and the umbrellas and the bowling pins were thrust out before him like an offering. Crosby walked to Dicky; Anne walked over to Emery.

Crosby's smile was bright and she was loud.

Hi Dicky!

Uh, hey Crosby.

I saw your Dad outside and he said you were gonna sing. You n' Emery. Like you always do.

I... uh, well, I dunno maybe—

You have to! If you don't it won't be funny. Emery doesn't dance around like you do.

Uhh-

Emery's not funny like you. If you're not there it won't be funny.

Then she walked away and Dicky stood crooked and smelled the bathsoap floating in the air as she passed. He stood back long enough to watch Anne walk away as well, then he weaved through those gathered between him and his brother the way skinny children can, even while holding their arms out straight.

Emery's eyes got wide and he smiled just a bit.

Ye got it already!

Uh huh.

Emery took hold of one of the umbrellas, and measured it like a ball player tests the weight of a new bat.

Wayne's gonna do his harmonica solo, so... it's you n' I again.

Uhuh.

'Singing in the Rain". We'll do it like we always do.

Yuh. Just like last year.

From the journal of Eva Parks (Griffin) Watts

Fri Apr 13 1934

A great shock to the neighborhood to learn Mr. Davis passed away suddenly at 8 o'clock in bed. He was at Guild last night and feeling and looking fine. He was in bed at the time. We have lost a kind & good friend.

Cleaned front hall today. Cloudy & damp with NE wind.

Sat Apr 14 1934

A nice day with temp 40 to 50 with South wind. In PM Ma & I went to Hyannis to get presents for Sarah. Drove home in a hurry to try and beat out what looked like a bad thunder shower. It proved to be wind, but around 9 we got the thunder shower. Ma slept with me.

Sun Apr 15 1934

A lovely day with temp 46 this morning & wind NW going to East.

Lu, Frank, & their children Norm & Lottie down for the day and called me up. Went in to see Emilie Davis a minute this AM. Mr. Davis died at Mrs. White's where they had been all winter & his body brought up to his own house this morning.

A Shanty Story

There were a dozen or so shanties along the shore of Aunt Lydia's Cove, all grey and old. Those to the north had taken to age worse than the others and were ramshackle and settling off their posts and onto the beach. They were larger than the shanties at Scatteree and there was room enough inside and along the boardwalks in between for men and their dogs, trawl tubs, flag buoys, groundlines, brine barrels and corrugated buckets filled with equal parts ice and bottles of Narragansett lager. There was word of a municipal pier, so the most haggard were left to the will of nature.

Allie stood and waited by the door of Howard Eldredge's shanty. He set lobster pots with Howard from the middle of May to October about a mile offshore on the Crab Ledge, where the bottom was roughest. It was a two-day soak for nearly every pot to fill with eight to ten lobsters: three- and four-pound beauties the color of new mottled bricks, flicking and reaching, all eyes and antennae. When the run of females struck they'd move the pots to the Bantams, or the Island Ledge some nine miles to the east, though sometimes the deeper water was not always better for there were times when a pot held only a single lobster, a great twelve-pound thing with a crusher claw the size of a black-iron skillet. They were worth about as much as an empty pot.

    Allie kept his share of their catch in lobster cars: large wooden pens built below the low water mark of Scatteree where they'd be fed and kept fresh by the tides. He sold to the Mattaquasson Hotel, and the Hawthorne and sometimes the Bars Inn, and there were private household accounts in his neighborhood of Old Harbor as well as the Guild Hall, and he gave to the Legion Hall on School Street and every Sunday night there was lobster at his own table. There was always lobster, so the only concern was a vessel and a market.

    Howard Eldredge walked downward in large steps in his short boots from his house on the Barcliff. Howard was part Aquinnah, of the old bloodline of the Gay Head tribes of Martha's Vineyard. His faded blue shirt made his skin look the color of old mahogany. His hands were together and palms-up, as if he were in supplication, or had rescued a baby bird. Howard was a large man, larger than most anyone on the shore. Howard pulled full lobster traps from the seafloor with one hand, carried a full tub of trawl on one shoulder, and held a beer can with only two fingers and a thumb. A Portugeuse long-liner from Provincetown once told Allie on deck that Howard had the spirit of a bear.

    Here ya go Allie. Hattie made donuts.

    Howard proffered some greasy paper with the donuts, and Allie grabbed them willingly. Hattie Eldredge cooked them in duck fat, and they were at their very best when the morning came very early, and you were dry and needed quick salt and fat in your system before heading out to sea.

Hattie pitched a fit 'bout an hour ago and she felt bad for makin' me late, so she packed me up with these for ya.

Hattie Eldredge was cursed with epilepsy, which Allie hadn't seen in the flesh until one day when he walked into Howard's kitchen unannounced. That day was one of those late spring mornings when the wind came up warm along the shore and Howard kept his front door open. Hattie was on the floor all strung out with her slim arms and legs tense and quivering in each direction of the compass, and her dark eyes turned up white. She was a sweet woman, always meek and smiling, and Allie thought it was an awful sight to see her the way she was on her kitchen floor. He froze.

Howard had sat quietly at the table with his coffee and the Standard Times open to the boxscore of last night's Braves game.

Hi Allie! It's okay. She'll be done in a minute.

Allie made quick work of the donuts and spoke with his mouth half-full.

She alright, Pop? We can cut bait anytime really.

Nah! It passed. Doc Keene says I just gotta make sure she's breathin' and not turnin' blue. He says all I can do is just kinda talk to her ya know, and that's what I did and she came out of it fine.

The way Howard dealt with his wife's affliction was a good testament to his temperament. He was a mild man for his size, and never raised his voice. Allie figured fellows of his size have that luxury. Allie figured the Lord would have to enact His mercy on the life of any unfortunate soul who had the will and audacity to make Howard angry.

The afternoon in August was still and humid and the air inside Howard's shanty smelled heavy of fish oil and blood; everything they touched seemed to have salt and sweat upon it. They stood with their backs-to, and their arms and elbows worked in similar arcs with their heavy knives as they sliced off cod heads and skate wings and threw them into a large wooden barrel that set between them half-filled with salt and ocean water. Great, heavy barrels, which they figured would fit one of Howard and three of Allie. The bait was best when it sat for a time and fermented in the summer sun. Outside and above the length of the shore, scavenger flocks of herring and greater black-backed gulls hovered in hundreds over the shallows, drawn hungry to the wretched stuff. The din of their incessant wailing lasted until nightfall. The odor was overwhelming for those unaccustomed to it. Those of a lesser constitution—summer folk, mostly—grimaced in disgust when the wind was right. The smell clung to flesh and hair and some lobstermen were sometimes not allowed into the house at night, and were sent immediately and without argument to the pump and basin with a towel and a bar of Fels-Naptha.

A Shanty Story

Charles MacKay was grey and old like the shanties. That day he was how he was on most days: drunk and disgruntled and old. He leaned back slightly as he walked, for balance, down the dirt road to Aunt Lydia's Cove, to the shanties; his face was puckered and his nose burst with bumpy grog blossoms. The paunch above his belt was bulbous and rum-filled. He tread carefully onto the boardwalk with his chin to his chest, and muttered to himself and to no one repeatedly, as he always did.

Prove it!

Charles didn't fish, or have a boat, or have much at all to do with anyone who worked the shore, but he'd half-stumble himself there usually once a week, unsteady and unimpressed with most of whatever he saw in the world that day. He managed to find the doorway of Howard Eldredge's shanty, which was near the last off the boardwalk, and he stopped, wobbled, and made half a bow.

Howard! Howard, what the hell's goin' on in here? Prove it, godammit.

Howard Eldredge turned from his work.

Whaddya want Charles? Eh? What's wrong with ye?

Charles took one intoxicated step inside and failed. He grabbed the plank-jamb of the doorway and leaned himself up against it.

Keep yer hands in yer pockets, you!

Howard pointed a gloved long finger out the door.

Why don't you just move along, MacKay.

Charles swayed and he squinted towards Allie, who had shown his back to him.

Christ, you, Allie Griffin. Best keep yer hands in yer pock-

Perhaps it was the heat or the horseflies. For Howard, enduring many hours of both had worn away the resolve needed to tolerate one Charles MacKay. Howard threw down his blade and turned again fast, and he grabbed Charles by the seat of his pants and by the scruff of his collar, as if he were a kitten destined for a burlap sack and a brick. Charles struggled not, and hadn't the time to react before Howard was upon him. With ease and accuracy, Howard tossed the old drunk head first into the pickle barrel.

The shanties were teeming with folk near the end of most days in August and that day Jake Worth sat in the sun with Rufus Nickerson. Jake in his black tie loosened and his sharp white shirt unbuttoned at the collar, and most everyone else in their slickers and high boots or low boots or high boots turned down low. Jake left work from Chase's Chevrolet on Old Harbor Road, and he and Rufus sat on two upended barrels. At their feet were discarded cherrystone half-shells and a few empty green bottles of Frank James beer.

Harvey Bloomer rinsed off his heaping fishboxes by the low water, the tide in flow. He breathed hard and the sweat ran down his face from beneath his sou'wester. He wore his

A Shanty Story

coat and his hat because the gulls were thick overhead and they hovered and waited for one of his dressed cod to fall off one of the mounded boxes. Harvey figured it better to sweat than be shit upon.

Wilmer Doane, hearing Charles MacKay and his scream, went off-course along one of the planks of the shantywalk and tipped near forty pounds of market codfish onto the beach and boardwalk. He kneeled and refilled the wheelbarrow, and the ember of his Chesterfield stoked in the cigarette holder between his profanity and front teeth.

Round Rueben Eldredge stood alone and wiped sweat from his face and his neck twice every minute. Rueben was quite short and very fat, and Allie swore that if he walked up and down the shore long enough his pockets would fill with sand. When out of earshot they called him Rollin' Rueben.

Charles MacKay righted himself from beneath the lobster brine and he cried out in sharp breaths like an old woman. He flailed and foundered and fell again below the brine. When he got a foothold, he stood and reached out with both hands, looking like a shriveled and sodden lost child in the dark. He found the rim of the barrel and began to circle it, hand over hand, again, and again, and again. The brine sloshed like a pale stew around his waist. His eyes were shut tight, blinded by the sting of fish slime and sea salt. Scum and scales and bits of dead fish clung to every inch of Charles MacKay.

He went around that barrel—hand over hand—for a very long time.

Damn you Howard Eldredge! Where the hell's the end of this fence?

From the journal of Eva Parks (Griffin) Watts

Wed May 2 1934

Lovely warm day & very little wind. Temp up to 66. Warmest day yet. Cleaned dining room. Mae Martin died this morning.

Thurs May 3 1934

SE rain all day. Cooked & ironed. In eve Ma went to Manor to entertainment given by Legion. Willie took part with Gus Ellis as his partner. Ed went with Barb, & stayed to dance afterwards. Came home & brought Barb & Clara Baker in & had ice cream & cake which I had on hand. Elmer Emery died today.

Sun May 6 1934

Another day like summer with temp 70. Arthur, Hattie & Ellen down for day. In AM Ma, Ida & I went to cemetery & took flowers. Louise came down & brought Edith Burke to stay at Allie's while Eliz. in hospital.

Mon May 7 1934

A lovely day with clear No. wind. Eliz. baby born this AM at 3 at C.C. Hospital. Taken sick at 11 last night. Everything fine & weighed 7 lbs. A nice Boy, & name James Arlen.

1st of September 1939

Allie strode out the backdoor of the house on Stony Hill Road in his low boots and his son walked barefoot beside him. He walked in the rapid manner that boys of his age did in summer. The low road to Scatteree was still damp and dark from the night's rain and the mud caked the soles of the boy's feet. There were many footprints left upon the road behind him in the dust underneath the mud. The sky was bright, the real blue of morning, and the fields of long grass on both roadsides were wet from the rain. The sun turned the raindrops on the high dead grass to gold. Lyle Nickerson would arrive next week with his tractor and wagon to mow and thatch and bale the fields for hay.

The boy walked with an oar under each arm. Both were more than a foot taller than himself, if he stood still and straight and tall, and they wavered slowly up and down with the haste of his footsteps. He had the oars for the dory, and his bait of clams were set in a four-quart wire basket safe above the high water mark near the shanties. His father's dory set anchored at low water. All he needed were the lines, which would be his lines, for it was the first time he was to fish by himself in his father's dory and every fish he caught would be his alone.

Allie's shanty was the first onto the path that bore north where the road ended at the shore, one in a row of four which faced east in a crooked row. They were all relative in size, none with ninety-degree angles at their corners and each with uneven small windows and roofs all a different shade of the same drab color. The boy and his father walked past Rufus Nickerson's black Ford beachwagon and felt the sun reflect warmly off it. His was the only car anywhere, but of Rufus there was no sign.

At the waterline were near a dozen herring gulls, and the boy knew immediately they were about his basket of clams, which were spared the creeping tide but not the gulls. He dropped the oars and ran in panic. His father hated gulls near most anything and his fine mood would change quickly if the boy lost his bait to the gulls because the tide was up and over the flats and there wouldn't be any more bait for hours, and he wouldn't fish for the first time alone in his father's dory.

He charged the gulls, and waved his hands and arms disjointedly like a marionette.

YEAAAAAAAAARRRRRGGGGH!

The gulls picked and bobbed at the basket and dallied stupidly around it until the boy had them within near an arms length, but they had the quick second to scatter into the air with their heavy wings. They didn't fly away but hovered

1st of September 1939

upward on their heavy wings and cried and cursed and the boy almost did the same. He kneeled around the basket and looked at the crushed mess inside and the scatter of broken shells around it. He picked out those that were broken and as he did the toe of his father's low boot caught his periphery.

Ye didn't cover 'em did ye Dicky? Ye didn't cover 'em like I told ya.

Dicky didn't answer. He didn't want to give the wrong answer. He picked at the clams.

They didn't get 'em all, did they?

No.

What'll ye do with all them flounder, anyway?

Gonna clean 'em and peddle 'em. Nickel apiece.

Allie held out the lines he had prepared for his son and Dicky quit his picking and grabbed the neat-coiled lines.

No more than two lines at a time, ye hear?

Mmhmm.

An' ye don't leave any o' this aboard.

Mmhmm.

Peg yer oars in good before ye untie her.

Mmhmm.

How many times ye coil each hook when yer done?

Six times.

How's the water?

Warm. The harbor's always warm.

Not always.

Not when the tide's in. The water's colder when the tides in, right Dad.

Usually.

It's not always warm.

Ye tie her up good when yer done.

Eugene Eldredge stood by his power dory, which was up on posts, at the end of the shantypath. Eugene dressed as he did always: high boots and a heavy cap and long-sleeve shirt rolled up tight near his armpits. He had some Nordic blood in him for sure: he was tall and his hair was a shade of copper that bleached with the salt and the sun. The week prior Eugene was hand-lining cod not more than a mile off the beach and was said to have been billed by a swordfish, then made it back to shore with a hole in his dory the size of a glass-cut doorknob. By the look of it, the patchwork on the starboard side of the keel by the waterline was finished, and the bottom of the hull was evenly half-painted.

It was quiet, warm and windless and there was a pleasant absence of humidity and horseflies. There were sparrows on the grassy hillside, and far atop it the Leeds home was a solitary umber monitor overlooking Scatteree in its entirety. An American flag hung listlessly downward at full mast. The Leeds were from Philadelphia, and fine people.

Whaddya say Gene? Nice mornin' ain't it.

Eugene nodded and pointed eastward.

Bound ta get better. Vessel looks nice, Allie.

Beyond the boy and the dory, the anchorline stretched taunt off the bow of the *Virginia*. There were heavy white clouds from the south and they cast North Beach into shadow. The tide ran out and the reflection of the sky on the surface of the water was broken like a cracked mirror by the path of the current. There was no wind. No waves. The *Virginia* looked freshly bleached in the sun and she floated like a white-feathered arrow due south on the mooring.

The two fishermen stood and watched Allie's boy wade towards the dory.

The ocean floor got stonier about the time the water cleared the boy's knees. He slowed his slog and dug in his toes, and with each step the bottom dropped further and the tide rushed around his waist and upset his balance, and he dug his toes in deeper. He reached the small vessel and put the left oar in first easily, but the right hit the rail and struck the bottom of the wire basket; the basket tipped and the clams spilled out in singular crunches on the deck.

Awwwwwww…

The boy reached, hopped up, held, twisted, and up over last were his legs as long arches of ocean sprayed from the heels of his feet, and he fell into a heap amongst the oars and clams with a low thud.

Eugene's eyes were hidden by the shade of his cap but Allie saw his half-smile.

That's some sorta outfit ye got there Allie.

Allie dug out his pipe and dredged deep into his pocket for matches. His smile was wide around his very white teeth.

Somethin' else, ain't he?

Christ, ye ever feed 'em? Boy's gotta stand up twice t' cast a shadow.

Eats just fine. The dinner table's nothin' but a snap an' a snarl an' an empty dish.

They stood bemused, and pondered the slow process of Allie's boy in the dory. At first he struggled to straighten it against the current, but he found his back and rowed well and the dory slid ahead atop the water.

Dicky went north against the current and it took him a few minutes to get to Donham's wharf where he drew up the oars and set anchor off the bow. He peered over the port rail and saw clear downward almost thirty feet. Small russet blooms of seaweed floated by slowly, and below were the flounder blanketed atop each other—hundreds it seemed: a great dark brown mass lying atop the smooth white sand unmoving. He looked down fore and aft, to port and starboard, and saw only uneven pairs of eyes looking back at him. He baited the two hooks with clams and tossed them overboard.

Eugene watched the boy bait and toss and haul in those perfect two-foot flounder one after the other, each baited hook scarcely reaching bottom before they were taken. The boy could go on like he was going for a very long time; only in the ebb of the tide would the flounder stop feeding.

Eugene checked his watch. He figured if the boy could last five hours, the flounder would.

What's he ever gonna do with all them flounder?

Clean 'em an' peddle 'em he says. Nickel apiece.

Eugene pulled a cigarette from the bib pocket of his overalls and lit it. He lowered his head and crossed his arms and kicked the sand with a weather-beaten shoe spotted maroon with bottom-paint.

I 'spose ye heard it all have ye Allie?

What's that Gene?

Eugene raised his head and his eyes stayed in shadow and he exhaled quick jets of smoke from his nose. He bit tobacco from his lip and spat.

Germany went into Poland I guess 'bout quarter o' nine this mornin'.

The smell of salt was strong everywhere suddenly. It settled in with the tide and the heat of a day in late summer. Allie shoved his hands deep into the pockets of his baggy trousers. His jaw worked and the pipe moved up and down between his teeth.

Well…

He looked down and took the pipe from his mouth and with his low boot, kicked the sand too.

…I guess I'm not surprised.

Smoke whistled low from between Eugene's lips.

No. Neither surprised am I.

Allie looked out at his boy who looked very small all alone in the dory, not much more than a pointed head with a scruff of blonde hair above the rail. It was his birthday this coming week, he would be ten, still young, and school would start after that. His brothers were much older.

That's bound t' change lots 'round here, Gene. Might mean war.

Eugene nodded once.

Yuh. Pretty sure it means just that.

From the journal of Eva Parks (Griffin) Watts

Mon May 15 1934

Rained in AM but cleared later in the day. SW wind and temp around 60. Mrs. Bloomer died this morning.

Ed worked on shrubs this PM. W & I worked out after supper.

Dicky up and washed up & had bread & molasses before going home to bed.

Tues May 16 1934

Rained most of the day & all eve. Ed & Clara walked home from town in the rain & had to dry off in the kitchen. Nantucket Lightship sunk by Olympic in the fog in night. 7 lost.

Thurs May 18 1934

Perfectly calm all day but rather cloudy. Allie got 800 lbs of fish. Got $12 for them. Dicky up with us most of the day and after supper up again for his "chores" & bread & molasses & cookies & milk.

Fri May 19 1934

SW wind this AM & temp 56. Sun out. Edith feeling miserable with her cold & may have to go home.

Sat May 20 1934

Another nice day, NE Wind. I went to hospital & took Ma along and we brought Eliz. & Jimmie home. He is the sweetest thing. Edith's cold so bad we did not dare let Eliz. go home for fear of catching it, so I slept in the upper hall, with him on a pillow with two chairs. Eliz. in middle room. Got along fine.

How it Was, Early

There was light from the small lamp by the kitchen door. Otherwise the house was dark, and made darker by the heavy green blackout curtains drawn across every window. Allie walked out his door and looked over his back field and along Old Wharf Road downward, and towards the water. He saw well in the dark. He lit his pipe, and three roosters and twenty hens in the backyard henhouse rustled and clucked at the flame. The air—as it was by the water in May when it was dark and cool in the morning—was full of stars and smelled of salt. Old Harbor had nearly shed its winter drab, and Allie could smell the greening of the land with the salt.

The wind blew the sheets on Doris Long's clothesline, which were a visible grey in the dark. Doris had herself a small laundry service during the lean years. She'd shuffle sideways along her lines for most of the day: pick the pins, fold it over her right arm, drop the bundle into the wicker basket on the grass by her feet and kick it expertly to keep her hands free. Allie found that when the morning was dark, the quickest and most accurate tool for wind direction in Old Harbor were the bed-sheets of Doris Long.

Dicky walked out onto the porch and the sound of the door as it closed behind him was loud and the chickens clucked again. The boy was tall and thin and he slouched forward. His clothes hung loosely around his neck and waist. He tried to stand up straight for his father, but one eye was heavy lidded and the part of his hair stood up straight like the tail of a partridge.

Mornin'.

Ya'll set?

Mmhmm.

Get yer jacket. She'll be a chilly ride out.

The boy turned back inside the house for his jacket, then father and son walked towards the shanties in the dark. By the lower curve along Old Wharf Road they saw the orange light burn outward from Herbert Baker's kitchen window, like the color of many low lit candles. In the early morning Bert was usually at his table—at the seat with his back to the door so he could look out to the water—and breaking his fast with a hard-boiled egg and Irish coffee. Bert was the sole proprietor and employee of Crescent Novelty Manufacturing Company, and a massive six-wheeled transport the color of marsh mud set in front of his workshop, with the letters USN stenciled in white upon each door.

At Scatteree and over the ocean the sky was an opaque indigo color as the morning began in darkness and the stars faded. Ted Loveland's loden green Ford set parked in the shanty lot. As was required by law--and Ted being the air raid warden--the headlights were dimmed, with their topmost half blacked-out with paint. Allie walked toward it, and moved his son away and towards the shanties with a hand to the back of the boy's shoulder.

Ye go down and get the bait aboard.

Pipesmoke and Ted's elbow hung out the open driver's window. Allie took his pipe from his coat pocket.

Christ, Ted, some early ain't it?

Ted Loveland took the pipe from his mouth.

Figured I'd do a drive about. Make sure all's as dark as it should be.

Allie doffed his sou'wester and scratched the scalp under his brown hair.

Looks t'be a grey mornin' too.

Yuh. Still, somethin' nice about drivin' around with the heat on yer feet an' the window down.

Yuh. I figure if I can't go out and make fifty, I'll make five.

What's with the satchel, there, Allie?

Oh. This here. Mail. Pollock Rip Lightship. They'll call ye over if you're runnin' passed. Told them the other day I'd pick it up for 'em n' this' just what they send down for the out-goin'.

Ted cleared his throat.

I see Bert's got the Navy at his door.

Mmhmm.

How often they come, would ye say?

More often than not, as of late. Bert tole me he's got a government contract. Makin' aircraft spindles.

Hmm.

Bert's talented, Ted. He's got a patent for a shingle bracket.

You walkin' the outer shore this evenin' Allie?

Yuh, I think they give me n' Joe from about the station there north t' the Orleans line. My sister Eva's got that camp now just this side of the station. Figure we'll retire there afterwards.

Been a few sightings from the night crew in Orleans. So they say.

Hmm. I say Ted: it's hard to see much of anything at night.

Mmhmm.

I ain't sayin' they didn't see what they saw. Hell I'm pretty damn positive I seen a periscope once this spring.

Allie rifled through his coat pocket for matches.

Ye can smell oil on the water when the wind's down. If it's up, well, there's these calm pools on the swells. There's boats sunk out there for sure, Ted. Far out past the Figs.

Ted's face looked grim with his pipe downturned like his bottom lip.

How it Was, Early

Far out. Still close. They found a rubber raft off some Nazi vessel. Print on it all in German.

Allie lit and stoked the remnants of last night's tobacco. He looked to the east.

I don't know if you've been over there Ted, but I've been over there, and back again. An' I tell ye: that's an awful lot of ocean t' cross.

Dicky loaded the bait into the dory with the oars, then stood by the shanty door. His father had tacked a heavily salted filet of market cod on the ridge by the door. He picked at it and put several bits in his mouth as he waited.

The boat was fueled, the bait was aboard and Allie made a course for the Great South Channel. Past the bar and due east-south-east of the Pollock Rip Lightship it was fifteen miles. With the weather how it was and the tide running south it would be an hour and a half to get there.

Dicky stood by his father, and was glad for his jacket. He knew of the mornings aboard the vessel when the wind was up and the blast of it stayed between your ears as the waves against the hull sprayed seawater into your hair, no matter which way you turned your head. It was a long day on the water, a rare day when he didn't want to be aboard with his father. When he was younger, he was made to stand close and to know where to move about so that he would never be at his father's back. It was only recently that father let him work the lines and be kept busy alone with the bait and the joyful hammersmash of the conch shells.

Some days there were Right Whales. When the whales began their dive to the deep water, and their vertical tails struck the surface, Allie told his son the only sound as loud were the 90 mm cannons he fired aboard the *North Dakota* in the war. Sometimes there were Right Whales, and rogue waves, and always haddock.

There was an ease to which you hauled when fishing for haddock. They had a soft lip, and if the hook wasn't deep into the jaw there was a chance it'd break off. Allie used two lines and fished back and forth between them both: a lead tied a few feet from the hook, and two more feet of line attached, and two feet more to another. He'd strip the haddock, bait the hook and toss the first line over again, then move onto the second, bait and toss and back to the first, and the fish unending. He worked back and forth like that for hours, and when Allie had a mate aboard the two from a distance looked as if they were dancing.

Five or six boxes of haddock were a good day. But the boy wasn't strong yet, so they wouldn't get five or six boxes.

The *Virginia* approached the exit to the harbor where the Coast Guard surf boat lay anchored with a lone sailor aboard. He waved when he spotted the *Virginia*, and Allie ran the vessel alongside. The sailor was young, and he tipped the cap of his uniform.

Where ya headed this morning?

Inshore. Figured maybe the Crab Ledge.

How it Was, Early

Do you know if there's gonna be anyone out there with ya?

Well, none I know of. Price a' pound the way it is, I don't s'pose there'll be too many out. Not sure I'll be too long m'self t' be honest.

Well... keep your eye out for me. For anything.

Allie nodded.

Will do. Anything particular?

The sailor paused, and smiled, unsure. His voice lowered in the dark morning, but Allie heard well in the dark.

Anything at all.

From the journal of Eva Parks (Griffin) Watts

Sat Jan 5 1935

Calm, and lots colder this AM down around 12 when I came down @ 730 but warmed up fast & up to 40 in PM. Cleaned up downstairs this AM & cleaned up kitchen in PM. Phil down to stay all night as Ida & Joe gone to Evelyn Jones to party & others all away. Joe's costume a work of art, but words fail me when trying to describe it. Half man & half woman. Allie went trawling today & sold their fish to dealers-- steak cod as high as 11 cents lb. Dealers from all around after them, as no fish anywhere now, & dealers bid for their fish on the shore.

Tues Jan 8 1935

Another warm day. Temp 46 this morning, & now 56 at 9 AM. Lots of ground fog & boats unable to get out. Sun shining through and no wind. Temp went to near 60. In middle of AM it cleared some and some boats went out, but foggy outside. Allie & Bill Lovering got about 500 lbs, which they sold & got $40. All boats came in except Charlie Peters & his pardner. They had no compass and got caught in the fog and unable to get in. They went out farther than the other boats, and nothing to guide them. W went to chicken pie supper at Legion Hall.

Wed Jan 9 1935

Another day of thick fog, and temp 58. Some rain. Everyone anxious about Charlie Peters. Coast Guard boats from C.G. stations here, and from Woods Hole, Provincetown, & Boston in fog searching for them all day. At night time no word.

Thurs Jan 10 1935

Charlie Peters & Albert Young were found by a steamer around 3 this AM when the fog lifted. Were taken aboard and had to be taken to Phila., steamers port because C.G. unable to get to steamer to take them off. Their boat towed in next day.

Poured all day & we went to Guild.

Emery's Tale

It was nineteen days across the Pacific Ocean. The assault transport was made to hold Higgins boats and twelve-hundred men. There were twenty-five hundred or more aboard, and Emery was one of the many that sat uncomfortable and crowded amid the stacks and overhangs. Everywhere he walked on ship there was someone in front of him, behind him, or one to each or either side. Chow was only twice a day because of the crowd. It was amusing how the war was over but even on the ride home you had to hurry to stand in line to wait a long time to eat. He and a few shipmates stole bread from the galley which was baked on board and was bland and heavy but smelled wonderful in the ovens. There were five hundred Marines on board and one of them had brought two monkeys with him from the Philippines and Australia. The best parts of the long blue days were watching the monkeys chatter at each other atop the great masts of the vessel, climbing up and down between one, the other, and back again. The Pacific was blue and endless and they were alone surrounded by it. Close to eighteen months ago westward from Hawaii they had LSD convoys and four destroyers in escort to detect enemy submarines. The great grey warships, and the symmetry of their wake and formation broke up the blue. There was always something to watch, and it had kept Emery's mind off his destination.

Nights were still the most uncomfortable: the bunks were stacked so tight together that Emery could not sleep on his side, and in order to turn over he had to get out of the bunk completely. He overheard a story from some nervous fellow--who chain-smoked cigarettes now that he could--about how he tried to sleep but still heard the land-crabs from the islands: crabs the size of coconuts and the horrid scuttling noise they made in the dark, like dead autumn leaves in the wind across an empty road. It was hard to sleep when he closed his eyes and heard those crabs in the dark. Nights were bad for some of them.

Emery knew it would end; they all did. There was never word of defeat. The 112th Naval Construction Battalion reassured themselves with words like *The Golden Gate in '48*. On Tinian it was humid and the temperature often reached one hundred degrees. He was told to watch for snakes on the islands, but he never saw any. There were mosquitos everywhere as they plowed haul roads through the fields of sugar cane to construct airfields and runways out of the abundant coral, nine thousand feet long, for the B-29 Superfortresses that were flying from the 'States, brand new in their thousands. It was tedious maintenance and engineering with the coral, which would wash away easily in the Pacific downpours. At night there was guard duty around and about the water wells because the enemy was starving and came out at night to forage for food and water.

David Howes sought Emery out on Tinian. David--who was a carpenter back home and now a warrant officer in the Navy, and was a friend to Allie, who called him Dooley--was on leave from the Aleutian Islands and back home. He had spoken with Allie and Eliz and informed them he was destined for Tinian. He promised Eliz that he'd check in on her boy. When he drove up in a Jeep, Emery felt an odd homesickness, seeing a familiar face when they were both as far across the Earth as they could be from home. He didn't know whether to salute him or say *Hey Dooley!*

David was hardly out of the Jeep before he was back in and away, his provincial duty fulfilled.

Don't dog it, Griffin.

Okinawa was the staging for the invasion. They were near Buckner's Bay, on the south side of the island, where much of the fighting was. They built field hospitals and every other day there was rain, and the work slowed. Emery had the fortune of being the only man in his company who could actually run a boat, and it was a willing duty and he became coxswain of the Higgins boat that ran between the island and any anchored craft that needed men ferried ashore.

The night was different. During the day they worked their bodies, and the night patrols overworked their wits. Always there were aircraft overhead with the open turbine engines like a constant thunder between dark and daylight. There was the company of gunners on mop-up duty in the darkness: the skilled southern Negroes--all from Alabama--who had been at Guadalcanal, and the Marshall Islands, Peleliu and Tarawa. Each shelling was four hours at night along the high ground of caves where the enemy hid.

Storms were abundant in the Pacific, and the familiar crash of waves on the shore sounded like pavement under the distant march of many heavy boots. Two days before they were to be discharged from the island a typhoon hit and the wind took away Emery's tent and every other set of clothing he owned.

When they made port in San Francisco it was four days in Treasure Island, days Emery and the rest spent in line at one of the three Navy receiving stations, most of the time to sign papers, and to find and pay for tickets for the trains that left for every place in the country that everybody needed to be. From San Francisco to home it was six days in travel compartments that were day coaches with no beds, through Cheyenne, and the mountain pass to Ogden. The Rocky Mountains came out of the ground like some wonderful mistake of nature: a rough hewn gateway to the unending low country of the Midwest.

The train was overfull with soldiers who could do no more than sit up straight so as to not touch elbows with the men packed on either side, or touch the knee of the other in the seat across, and all amid the smell of soot and sweat in uncomfortable proximity. It was no better by the window, where the dissipated contrail of coal smoke came through with the warm air off the plains. Emery found it difficult to breathe at times. The train soot was everywhere, and when he put his hand down upon any permanent surface it came away black.

He remembered Kansas City, but the remaining stops were nameless, anonymous country where the train was refilled with water and coal. Amid the tedium he thought of home, before wartime, and what he had done when he left it. At school, when he was seventeen and as class president read aloud the note Fred Devlin had written to the class from Guadalcanal. Fred was eighteen, and so were Kenny Nickerson and Paul Robertson and Al Durkee and Warren Sampson, and all were taken out of school by the draft board and sent to war before they could graduate. Emery needed written permission from his father.

He wondered what home looked like now that there was peace in the world.

The train reached Boston and emptied at its final eastern destination. Emery exited bedraggled, and followed a crew of fellows he didn't know to the supply depot to re-outfit themselves with freshly pressed naval khakis. And he followed again when he heard one of the fellows had a brother at the Quincy firehouse and there were showers, the first for almost ten days. Emery saw himself in the mirror, tanned, and nearly black with the dirt above the collar of his neck, and around his eyes, mouth and nostrils. He didn't look healthy, but when it was clean he saw it was the same face.

It was quarter to five in the late afternoon when the bus from Hyannisport stopped at the short wall by the lawn of the Methodist Church. Emery took three steps downward onto Main Street with his cross-shoulder satchel and his sea bag. The lights were on inside Puritan Clothing, and he saw Benny Shufro through the glassfront. He went in without hesitation, and the inside was warm and smelled distinctly of leather and the unsung pleasure of washed fabric. It was so quiet, and the false light bothered his eyes. He looked for a place to sit in the case he needed to.

Benny Shufro stood up straight from his half-bent position and half-smiled in recognition, the other half in unfamiliarity.

Well. Emery! Boy, where are you comin' in from?

It was nice to hear someone talk without having to raise their voice above the constant rumble and hiss of the bus, and the iron roar of a transcontinental trainride. The quiet was cathartic, and so was the sight of Benny.

Okinawa.

Benny went still for a moment. Then he nodded and made for the lights by the door. There was a click and the store went dark and the evening dusk felt better on his eyes.

Well, I'm closin'. You sit tight and I'll drive ye home.

No thanks, Mr. Shufro, I've—

Mr. Shufro came up and shook his hand.

Lookit ye! C'mon now! Can't have ya walkin' home to yer mother alone.

He took hold of Emery's sea bag.

No question. Just need my coat and keys.

Benny drew drapes across the windows and shut off some back lights and Emery walked out ahead of him as he rattled the keys in and out of the lock of the front door.

Did ya see the church?

Mr. Shufro pointed upward at the Methodist church.

Steeple came down in the hurricane last year.

Emery noticed the white squared-off column of the church where the steeple was missing.

I heard New England got hit, but that's all.

Emery, the whole town looked like it had been turned upside down and shaken like a cocktail.

Emery pictured his father standing by the front window, arm crossed with his pipe, watching the storm and the wind and the limbs on the large oak, and what resulting element of nature was strongest. He'd stay awake all night if the storm lasted through.

Benny led them to his car.

Ye spoken to yer ma or dad?

No. Not yet. I've sent word, every so often.

Emery had to think for a second whether his youngest sister was three years old or four.

My sister Joyce ain't gonna know who I am.

He passed Jesse Tuttle's butcher shop and The Sign of the Surf, Doctor Keene's office and the Congregational Church. Onto Old Harbor Road was New England Telephone, and Roscoe Gould was parked there for his night shift until morning, when he punched out and drove the morning bus to school. Near Depot Road lived the Corrigan's who had seven or eight children, but Emery had been gone for two years so there were probably more. Across the road was the Duncreevan Inn, and down Highland Avenue was his mother's church. There was Earl Hunt's funeral parlor, and Chase's Chevrolet. Down Thayer's Hill he smiled at the four steep steps at the end of the Bloomer's yard, four steps that every Bloomer child fell down while rushing to the bus stop. Sidney and Emily White's place was beyond that, set in where the schoolhouse was when his father was young. His Aunt Ida's field was unmowed and half-dead. Emery suddenly remembered that day in the field when Frankie Hutchings was warming up his swing with the two baseball bats. Matt Plum was Arlen's age, and he lived on the estate out by the Oyster River, and played ball with the boys from Old Harbor all summer when he wasn't at school in New Hampshire. Matt was only a fair hitter but he had a great arm and caught every poor ball thrown at him. That day he bent over behind Frankie to pick up his mask and Frankie swung over his shoulder and the bat split Matt's head with that uncommon sound of force against skullbone. Matt fell to the ground and stayed on the ground. Poor Frankie's voice cracked as he cried out at the blood that poured over Matt's hair and skin suddenly, and very red in the sun. The brothers and the boys carried Matt to the house and Eliz. washed his head out calmly in the sink and waited for Doc Keene, who stitched him up without issue.

Benny stopped in front of the old homestead. It all looked familiar. Still he wondered if it was the same place.

It was good to be home again and alive.

From the journal of Eva Parks (Griffin) Watts

Wed Jan 23 1935

Temp 28. Strong NE wind, developing into worst blizzard in years, with snow sleet & a gale. W went to Boston to a hearing, and Ma & I alone here. Grew cold during night--light went out. Got up Thurs AM found temp 18, and no electricity on, so no heat, & radiators cold. House was some cold, but got kitchen fire going & kept warm there. Lights were fixed by 9:30. A broken wire on Thayer's Hill. Stayed cold all day. Roads blocked down Cape, & no connections with trains between here & Hyannis for the day. Grew colder at night. No Guild.

Fri Jan 25 1935

Zero this morning. But clear--went up to around 18 during day. Ma & I went to Guild it being postponed till today on account of Storm. W came home from Boston on 1:30 train & went to town meeting in eve. Town turned down Kate Gould's bequest of land for park.

Tues Jan 29 1935

Temp the AM around 28 calm, and a thick fall of light snow til 10 AM. Temp at noon up to 40 dropping to 32 by mid PM. Rigged up in pants etc and went out coasting with the gang on Stevens Hill for afternoon. Lots of fun. Ida, Barb, Sarah, Grace Dreghorn, Doris Long, Grace Doane, Clara Baker, Alta Hopkins, Ina Regan, Bob Dreghorn, Joe, Milton Baker, Sidney White, every kid in neighborhood, some from downtown & C-port.

30th of October 1950

There was wind and rain that morning but the stormclouds moved out like grey horses over the northern shore to the sea. In town the trees were hassled by the wind and rain, and there were damp blankets of dead yellow pine needles on the roads and lawns and roofs of houses. Autumn was wet and grey, and in the old tradition the best season of the year for fish.

Allie made his northern course for home from the Mussels, some eight miles south of the harbor, with his son and fifty boxes of dressed haddock. When they passed the Stonehorse Shoal lightship off the south tip of Monomoy she looked alarmingly red atop the water. Her horns sounded out low and clear, to warn of the fog ahead.

EeeeeeeeerroooOOOOOOwumpwump!

It was a straightforward course to the harbor but the ride was made slow by the waves: eight and ten foot swells ponderous and unbreaking, left in the wake of the storm. Autumn fog was common if the ocean was calm, or if the wind blew in from the east. The white and grey nothingness lay ahead of them, like sliding into and under some helpless curtain pulled downward over life itself. Yet it rendered all captains fearful, and those unwise were surrounded, and lost.

Allie had only his time and his compass in the fog, and with the bothersome waves a slow uneasiness crept forward from the lowest part of his mind. He looked sternwards, at his load of fresh haddock shining like piled silver. It was a strong market, and with luck he'd get an extra cent and a half per pound.

Dicky, I think it best we plug the scuppers.

Dicky stood tall in the bow. He'd finalized his tenure in the Army Reserves, and hadn't enough enlistment time to go to the war in Korea. He returned home, to fish. It was instilled into his blood by his father, redoubtable as the Catholicism bound to him by his penitent mother. Both were not just ingrained, but innate. Dicky knew of fog, and of how to stand tall amoung the swells. The afternoon was warm but still he wore a jacket, which looked heavy and poor-fitting on his thin shoulders. He walked slow and stable on his long legs along the rail, as the *Virginia* dipped down low and heaved upward again. He moved to the stern and plugged the scuppers in the transom behind the fishboxes, then to the pilot house behind his father.

Allie brought his speed up; the waves ran south with the outgoing tide. He looked out the starboard-side window to the sky and saw very little; the fog was heaviest and warm closer to shore and it dampened everything everywhere and beaded like dew on the windows. A column of sunlight broke through a few degrees off the bow, and turned the fog an off-white, like steam over pre-boiled water. It was odd weather, with the high-course tides at such extremes that week with the moon, and the white fog and the waves. The stern broke free slightly on the down turn of the waves despite being kept low in the water with all that haddock.

Allie kept a disquieted eye to his compass.

Keep yer eye out.

Can't see nothin' out those windows.

Dicky returned to the bow.

Never seen the fog as... bright as it is!

The fog neither thickened nor broke apart. Allie watched his compass; there was nowhere else to look. Then an uncomfortable clench in his gut rose up out of him with a disconsolate breath. A sudden break in the fog revealed the weather station atop Morris Island, and Allie knew his time was off. Not far off, but enough to stir his confidence. The fog swallowed them again.

The entrance to the harbor was close ahead. The tide rose and fell in only ten to twelve feet of water outside the harbor due to Pollock Rip Shoal. The furious north/south current of the tides cut away incessantly at the outer beach, and each season the entrance to the channel over the bar shifted stage-like southward. Similar shifting would occur after a three-day blow, all those changes unknown. To navigate over the bar and through the channel into the harbor was difficult in the finest hour of clear and windless afternoon.

Allie adjusted his speed and his time again. He trusted the compass and the *Virginia* made it over the bar slowly, riding atop the swells as best she could. Dicky moved again from the bow to the pilot house as they crossed into the harbor; the smell of the shore was strong and comfortable in the fog: a familiar, faintly rotten blend of cast-up seaweed and hollowed crab chitin. The land looked most welcome in a life on the water in the fog, with the stern low in the water with near one ton of haddock.

Father and son smoked cigarettes, and the trepidation and the fog began to fade.

Allie kept a steady time, and the swells fell and the fog burned off the further he made his way up the harbor. Another odd column of sunshine poured downward overhead, like some divine spotlight brighter than the day itself, turning the moisture in the air to silver dust.

There Dad, look! There's something all in the water. It's…

Empty trawl tubs appeared out of the haze floating upside down atop the water. There was air still up under them, and they floated, and one came close and nudged the bow and scraped slowly along the *Virginia's* starboard side.

Scrrrrrrrrrrrrrrrrrrrrrrrrrrrrrrrt.

30th of October 1950

White and red flag buoys followed the tubs, bobbing with their tethers still in half-coiled loops on the surface. They floated into view, passed them by, and disappeared into the fog behind.

Then upon the water came the fish: hundreds and hundreds of fish dead on the water, like a pathway of empty spirits razed from the dark bottom of the ocean. They covered the rolling ocean like paving stones.

The air was unmoving; the storm had taken all breath of wind out to sea with it. The only sounds were the muted diesel breath of the motor and the soft patter of dead fish against the hull.

Allie didn't slow until he heard a ship's bell ring out ahead to his starboard side, and the red saltworn hull of the *Jeanie S* emerged from the blur of the fog. He saw Vincent LeBlanc near the bow looking far over at the water and the dead fish, both hands holding tight to the rail. Vincent's shirt had once been a red-plaid but was worn and faded pink, and the cuffs were rolled up past the hard-marble muscles of his forearms.

John Stello was the young captain of the *Jeanie S* and he kept his vessel moving slow, wary of his load of haddock in her stern and the dying swells. His black bib oilskins were unable to cover completely his barrel chest. His big round face had a slack expression to it, and the look in his eye was clouded by the damp upon the lenses of his eyeglasses.

Allie! What in hell's goin' on here?

The two vessels drifted together down the harbor.

Nothin' good I'd say.

This weather. The waves. I was close to thinkin' I'd not make it over the bar.

Allie watched the scatter of dead fish float past and then to the overflowing number of haddock in John Stello's stern boxes; how clean they looked with their distinct lateral black Godsmark.

Johnny, yer low in the water.

Yuh.

So am I.

Yuh. I think it best we unload this catch.

Yuh. I think it best we might.

At the pier was a low stirring of men: the Ford police wagon drove up and out of the lot at some speed. Doc Keene was without a jacket and sat on the rear gate of his car and turned down the cuffs of his white shirtsleeves. John brought the *Jeanie S* portside to the pier and the *Virginia* followed. There were two other vessels in early from the fishgrounds, with boxes filled and silver. Standing over all of them was old Stanley Bishop the fishmonger: squat and strong in his black flat cap, boots and sweater, and with an old breed's strength loaded iced fishcrates with ease into the rear of his box truck.

30th of October 1950

The shore was shadowed by the seaclouds, and there was an unusual quiet for the number of men about. It was Ralph Long who came toward them first, limping like he did along the edge of the pier and packed a Pall Mall cigarette against his Zippo lighter. Ralph was dark and unshaven and his hat was up atop his forehead; he looked to have sweat a great deal--his old green sweater was damp across his shoulders and chest. He stopped to grab the sternline when it was within grabbing distance. Allie waited for Ralph's eye, but Ralph just looked away, and over him and the water.

What's the story Ralph?

Ralph stopped packing and lit his cigarette and took one long gentle pull as if that were a question he didn't have an answer to.

Found Roy Larkin floatin' there inside the harbor, Allie. Me n' Lou. Floatin' there dead in all that mess.

Ralph, where's Archie?

Ralph shook his head. He could not answer that question either. His words were monotone and cracked like his voice-box was giving out.

'O course Louis wouldn't allow 'em on board. I leaned over the rail y'know t' try to hold 'em up but... I dunno. I take it ye saw how it was.

Yuh. Weren't good.

Louis radio'ed 'em in, though.

That's good.

Louis radio'ed 'em in Allie. He's like that. Christ I couldn't say nothin'. It's his vessel.

I know Ralph.

They looked along the row of vessels at the pier and saw Louis far ahead and all there was of him was a shadow leaned against the pilot house, with his head down and his arms crossed. In his right hand was the receipt of payment for near one ton of haddock.

Doc, he worked on Ralph best he could. Awful with him... poundin' on his chest like that. All us standin' around 'em just watchin'.

He smoked hastily, as if his time was running out on the habit.

But that's how we found 'im. He was like that when we found 'im, Allie.

I know Ralph.

Archie musta lost his time. The fog. The waves.

Allie took his pipe out of his jacket pocket and knocked the bowl absently against his palm. He held it up to his chin.

He was pickin' up a new car today. His first new car. He said so yesterday.

Hmm.

30th of October 1950

I say, Ralph, they musta pitch-poled. Got on the wrong side o' the waves and pitch-poled.

Hmm. Yuh.

Bow would've driven right under, n' the stern of her would... well...

Larkin got his boots off.

He did?

Goddammit Allie he got his boots off. Musta known there was trouble.

Hmm. It'd happen quick...

Yuh.

Hmm. Shame. Poor Roy. Good on a boat he was.

He was.

Ralph Long walked away with his head down and the smoke from the cigarette between his teeth floated over both his shoulders. Chief Eldredge moved by Ralph and put a hand to his shoulder as he passed. His head moved all around as if he couldn't find something he was looking for, and he rubbed his hands and clapped them once together hesitantly as if not to disturb the low aspect about the dock. The chief took uncomfortable steps towards Allie, his son and his vessel.

Ye talked to Ralph.

Mmhmm. There's gear all over the harbor, Chief. Just inside the bar. Ye couldn't do nothin'. Not with the waves. Not with all yer catch aboard.

The Chief nodded, tried to half-smile, failed, and walked away.

Allie secured the port-side bowline and when he turned Doc Keene stood above him. Doc didn't wear a jacket, and wore his shirtsleeves rolled. Allie didn't want to speak with Doc Keene—as cruel a notion as that was--for Doc was trustworthy and kind and the reposing drawl of his native Maine had the cadence of all good doctors. The wry lines on his face had hardened.

Y'know Allie: that man hadn't been dead for a very long time.

Allie didn't care to speak much more about the conditions of dead men.

Ye can't blame 'em Doc. Lot of 'em are like that. French-Canadiens. Them Scots up in Nova Scotia. Them Portuguese up Provincetown are worse n' any.

Those that had returned and sold had gone back to search, with others: Crayton Nickerson aboard his *Mildred N*; the Boudreau boys on the red-hulled *Bobby Louis*; Cobbie Nickerson off by himself, the way he liked it; Amon Liska on the *JARVON*, who made his way on deck better than most, and him born with only one leg; and Allie's nephew Ed Tucker aboard the *Falcon IV*, which was a new grey and would have been near invisible in the fog. It ended that evening when the

30th of October 1950

sky turned the color of a hurtful bruise, and the search found no sign of the *Catchalot*, nor of Archer Nickerson.

Allie hoped that Archie had gotten his boots off and they'd find him somewhere, and he wouldn't be another sad mystery like those others left unrecovered. He hoped that Archie got his boots off, otherwise he'd sand over and be lost to the ocean bottom, and they'd never find him.

The first stars blinked in the north as Allie set his course for Scatteree and for home with his son.

From the journal of Eva Parks (Griffin) Watts

Mon Mar 4 1935

Another lovely day & temp 26 at 7 AM. Light No. wind and a swell wash day, which I made the most of. Temp got as high as 60 in the sun. Peonies showing through the ground, also Daffodils & crocuses. Letter from Gracie mailed at Colon, Canal Zone. Jean & Ralph Sewell called in PM & told us they heard our Ed Tucker was to be put on Old Harbor C.G.S.

Was in to Ida's awhile in eve.

Rained at bedtime.

Tues Mar 5 1935

Thick fog and temp 44. Sun trying to break through. Got a phone from Dr. Worthing that Ed. passed all exams for Coast Guard & papers gone in. Now waiting to be called. Turned out to be nicest day yet, mild sun--wind out and temp going up to 62. Called on Mildred Robbins & saw her some improved. Ma & I went to Guild in PM. Grace Dreghorn & Evelyn Jones hostesses. About 65 there by eve., and played "Bingo" till 9 & then were entertained by a minstrel show directed by Evelyn Jones. Those taking part were Wayne & Bob Griffin, Phil Nickerson, Edward Baker, Constance Jones, Emily Ryder, Shirley Long. They gave us a full show, consisting of singing, dancing, piano solo & harmonica solo by Wayne, jokes by all. Solo tap dance by Phil, & three girls did tap dance together. All were blacked up, & in costumes.

18th of February 1952

Scatteree was set in shadow by the storm, and winter. The wind had formed small ice drifts against the bare trees and the dead grass in every field was bent slightly and frozen like knife edges. That autumn had passed sunny and near cloudless--an odd season--but frigid north winds came in late October. The ground dried and froze quickly, and the snow started Thanksgiving day. The boats had been up on the beach since December and were locked frozen on their posts. The harbor itself iced over on the new year, and other than a few ducks, there was nothing at all that season from the sea.

For two days there was a gale of wind. From dark clouds the snow fell hard and felt sharp in the gale, and could be heard in dull notes settling upon the ground. The type of day in winter when it seemed the dark came early from the cold.

Allie stood on the beach between Rufus Nickerson's shanty and his own, alone among the dories, drums and potstacks. He saw the glare of headlights flash against the outside of the two shanty walls. He turned and didn't recognize the vehicle, but saw it was Jimmy Allison, the caretaker out on Strong Island for the Potters. Jimmy exited the car but left the engine running and the headlights on. Jimmy wore his own foul weather gear and he walked from the shantylot onto the windswept beach. The half-snow glazed upon it like beerfroth on old dimpled glassware. The ice along the high-watermark had built up grey and sharp and ragged as it continued throughout the season to rebuild itself. It all looked painful to slip and fall upon.

Christ Allie what 'cha doin' out here in this mess!

Allie wore dark oilskins, and his sou'wester was pulled low over his eyes. The collar was up on his jacket, and all Jimmy saw of him was a nose and a pipe.

Whaddya say, Jimmy! What 'cha think of all this? We'd get inside the shanty t' watch but I'd lose the cussid door in the wind!

The two men absently huddled shoulder to shoulder.

I came across this morning Allie but I been keepin' an eye on her all day. Figured I could follow her best at Scatteree.

Th' whole family's been in front o' that upstairs bedroom window. Watchin'. Couldn't see through 'em all so I took a walk. Got a spyglass here in the shanty.

It just come on the radio there's two ships broken up. Two tankers. And the other's close.

They give names to 'em?

They gave one: the Fort Mercer. That's prob'ly the stern of her right there.

18th of February 1952

Across the harbor and North Beach they watched the stern of the tanker: colossal, broken, and subject to the surf. It disappeared into the grey broil of ocean wash, wind and the fall of wet snow. She was a dark shape in the grey, and she sank downward out of sight and rose up again, held in the crest of a wave so high the bulk overtopped the light of Old Harbor Station. The horn sounded, as it had all morning.

Whooooooooooooohoooohooohooo!

It took both of them to hear anything over the wind. Even between two shanties the flakes were like rapid tapping fingertips on the shoulders of their coats. Each kept a hand to their face to shield their eyes as the weather came at both men sideways.

What's the size o'them waves?

Allie found a place for his pipe deep within an inside pocket.

Some big. Could be thirty, forty feet, Jimmy.

She don't seem to be movin' one way or th' other.

Tides changin' course. It'll run to the south soon and bring her right back down the beach.

There was a gust suddenly and the shantywalls shook and both men braced themselves against them. The grey waves on the shore flattened and went white; there was that single low note across the water as if the ocean itself took a single slow breath.

The tanker went out of sight again as the storm broke against her. Another solemn wail of the horn shuddered over the wind and across the harbor.

Whoooooooooooooohooohooohooo.

It was a vacant sound. Absent of hope or desperation.

Gotta be someone workin' that horn, Allie.

Allie tried again with the spyglass.

Figure she's at least two, three hundred yards off the beach. Christ, she'll fetch up on Bearse's shoal, dependin' on how strong that tide runs.

The Guard's out somewhere. You'd wonder if the Station's got a vessel out.

Allie didn't answer right away.

Tide's gone the other way, Jimmy. They'll have a hell of a time makin' it across the bar.

What about Old Harbor Station?

Eh. They ain't got a vessel big enough. Them waves are thirty foot, Jimmy. The surge o' the tide. The wind. And dark's comin'. Them poor bastards.

Allie shook his head. The misery of it all caught him suddenly; what endurance he had chosen and dressed for left him. He collapsed the spyglass and put it back atop its place in the shanty. He secured the door twice, which was what he told himself he would do.

18th of February 1952

Come on up th' house Jimmy. I got some o' that daisy wine I bottled this summer.

Alright. Maybe get a last look out that bedroom window, eh?

Allie turned his back to the ocean.

Them poor bastards.

www.ingramcontent.com/pod-product-compliance
Lightning Source LLC
LaVergne TN
LVHW050045090426
835510LV00043B/3023